Praise For *7-Figure Formula*

"In typical Justin Michael-style, he delivers the exact framework, messaging, and mindset to follow to achieve success levels that everyone wants, but few attain. In a time where every out-of-work, ex-whatever is now a coach, peddling rehashed--often dubious-- advice they have seen online from other 'bros,' Justin holds nothing back from his verifiable successful work in the trenches, and supercomputer mind full of research he's done. This book could be a $20K course for consultants/coaches/solopreneurs and still be underpriced."

– Art Sobczak, author of "Smart Calling- Eliminate the Fear, Failure, and Rejection from Cold Calling"

"I'm always impressed by Justin's beginners mind. He shares all he knows in this book to help shortcut your learning."

– Ankush Jain, Transformative Coach, Business Mentor, Author & Speaker

"Justin has the power to transform your life—if you're ready to let him. He gave me a proven formula and blueprint that helped me launch and scale my coaching business to over $12K in my first month. His strategies work, and I'm living proof."

– Brandon Clauser, CEO, BC Sales Coach

"10/10—this book feels like peering through a keyhole into the art of the possible. The satirical and humorous tone makes even the most challenging concepts feel approachable and attainable, breaking down barriers and inspiring confidence. It's both motivating and transformative, revealing strategies and insights that would typically cost tens of thousands of dollars to access."

– Doug Rendler,
Sales Leader & Advisor, Fluence

"Think of Justin Michael as the espresso shot in a world full of decaf—focused, intense, and impossible to ignore. In Seven-Figure Formula, he serves up a bold recipe for building a seven-figure life with a side of inspiration and hustle. Get ready to wake up and get things done."

– Rich Habets, Founder,
Business Coaches Academy

"Becoming a solo consultant or starting your own business is both exciting and daunting. Justin's methodology and mindset for finding and winning new clients is phenomenally successful. His new book, 7-figure Formula, is a must-read for anyone with a great product, service or solution who now needs to crack the code on building profitable revenue."

– Tony J. Hughes, CEO,
Sales IQ Global

"Justin Michael has done it again—and this time, he's outdone himself. This book is a tactical powerhouse for any sales professional aiming to master their craft and become a 'Niche of One.' After working 1:1 with Justin, I replaced my entire

Salesforce earnings and went solo as a coach in just 30 days. If you're ready to put in the work, this book will compress a decade of learnings into one year—it did exactly that for me."

– Christian Krause, Founder & Head Coach,
The SaaS Sales Academy

"Justin Michael is ruthlessly authentic and brings decades of hard-earned expertise to the table. 7-Figure Formula is packed with practical strategies that cut through the fluff and get to what actually works. This isn't theory—it's a straight-talking guide from someone who's lived it and mastered it. For coaches ready to stop spinning their wheels, 7-Figure Formula is the real deal."

– Towsend Wardlaw, Founder,
(www.TheCoachsOperatingSystem.com)

"It might sound cliché, but Justin's 7-step method helped me replace my W2 income in just three months, allowing me to go full-time as a consultant. Since then, I've landed half a dozen clients who now pay me double what I earned consulting on the side—all for the same amount of work."

– Greg Larsen, Founder,
Catalyst Sales Consulting

"Justin Michael is the modern Q from the James Bond movies, and his books are the Aston Martins of the day. Volume 4 of his JMM series is both stirred and shaken to take the readers onto a transformational flight through magic walls towards mastering limitless client acquisition of modern solopreneurship."

– Gunnar Habitz, Author of Connect & Act,
Partner Manager at ActiveCampaign

"Justin has truly outdone himself with 7-Figure Formula—a masterclass on building and running a thriving solo consultancy. If you're lucky enough to work with him 1-on-1, you can expect a 5-10X return. Don't wait. Buy the book, absorb its insights, and take action. The path to success is right here."

– Mario Krivokapic,
Founding Partner @ Revenue Architects

"Justin has poured his heart and expertise into this book—it's like his living legacy. If you're a coach, advisor, or consultant wondering how the top 1% earn millions while you struggle, this book reveals the answers with striking clarity. When he decided to release this resource, once reserved for his highest-paying clients, I hesitated—urging him to protect it. But I realized a timeless truth: while many may read it, only a rare few will apply its gold. I'm proof of its power—at this writing, I just had a $148K week."

– Jonny Staker,
Founder/CEO at Vanquish

"In typical Justin Michael fashion, 7-Figure Formula is a highly engaging read packed with value. Justin pulls back the curtain to reveal the formula to supercharge your ability to acquire clients. This is THE book that every coach, consultant, or solopreneur needs to read!"

– David Hoffeld,
Bestselling Author of Science of Selling

"Justin lives his ethos—for being the top 1% of the 1%; his grind is still second to none. His process (which got me eventually reading and then devouring this book) is a practical lesson in how effective his methods are—super practical and laden with nuggets that provide immediate value. The book itself? An absolute masterpiece."

– David Lichtenstein, Co-Founder,
Superhuman Sales & Superhuman Ventures

"Justin's methods empower sales professionals to break through self-imposed limits and thrive in today's competitive market. If you're ready to launch your coaching, consulting, or advisory business, this book is your roadmap to attracting dream clients and building a business beyond your imagination. Having generated millions as a solopreneur, Justin has helped countless others, including me, create six-figure businesses in just months. Now, he's sharing it all in his latest book. Embrace it, apply it, and keep coming back to it—it's a game-changer. Thank you, Justin, for your life-changing guidance."

– Aaron Norris,
Global Sales Coach & Consultant

"Few mentors truly have the passion to help others succeed, but Justin is one of them. In this book, he lays out a powerful case for creating a business that helps people live wealthy, fulfilling lives. My advice: read it, take it to heart, and start believing in yourself—you're capable of more than you think!"

– Peter Strauss,
Global Sales Advisor,
Vparagon

"Justin Michael is revolutionizing modern sales with his innovative insights. Dive into his work, absorb the wisdom, and implement it boldly. Justin could have excelled in countless fields, yet he's chosen to share his brilliance with us through 7-Figure Formula. Thank you, Justin, for giving us your very best."

— Patrick Tinney,
Founder & Managing Partner, Centroid Marketing

"When I left my corporate coaching role, I was eager but overwhelmed by how to build a thriving business. Working with Justin changed everything. He showed me how to focus on creating clients, and within a month, I closed 3 in a single day, generating $38,000 and $10,583 MRR. His system gave me the freedom to scale up or step back when life demanded it, all without the stress of wondering where my next client would come from."

— Luke Harris, President,
Seacliffs, Inc.

"Justin Michael exemplifies true service, blending actionable strategies with profound insights on being—the core driver of success. His use of Ikigai principles—aligning love, passion, vocation, mission, and profession—is like discovering life's Holy Grail. With generosity and clarity, he empowers others to create and achieve possibilities. A truly excellent book!"

— George Stephen Shaw,
Financial Advisor

"The number 7 is historically linked to success. In this simple guide, Justin, as your co-pilot, shares his 'top-secret' seven-step framework to help you achieve your seven-figure dreams. He's done the hard work for you—now, you can fly solo. Let go of your limiting beliefs and focus on what should be our highest reward: Finding joy (and dollars) in helping others succeed."

— Frank Kohn, Principal,
High Value Strategic Advisors

"7-Figure Formula by Justin Michael is hands down the best book ever written on mastering client acquisition as a solopreneur. With bold, actionable strategies, it demystifies scaling your business and conquering impostor syndrome. This book gave me the clarity and confidence to stop overthinking, take action, and start closing deals. If you want to land premium clients and build a seven-figure consultancy, this is the ultimate must-read."

– Marc Periou, Principal,
MP Hunter Holdings

7 FIGURE FORMULA

Client Acquisition Secrets For Coaches, Consultants, and Solopreneurs

Justin Michael

JONES MEDIA PUBLISHING

7-Figure Formula: *Client Acquisition Secrets For Coaches, Consultants, and Solopreneurs*

Copyright © 2025 by Jones Media Publishing

All rights reserved. No part of this publication may be reproduced, distributed, or transmitted in any form or by any means, including photocopying, recording, or other electronic or mechanical methods, without the prior written permission of the author, except in the case of brief quotations embodied in critical reviews and certain other noncommercial uses permitted by copyright law.

Jones Media Publishing
10645 N. Tatum Blvd. Ste. 200-166
Phoenix, AZ 85028
JonesMediaPublishing.com

Printed in the United States of America

ISBN: 978-1-948382-94-6 paperback

Ready to multiply your sales results?

Get all the resources and bonus material for this book and the JMM series in one place.

Download the book resources here free:
SalesSuperpowers.com/bonus

Contents

Introduction: How to Get Clients, Make Bank, and Still Have a Life xv

Section I: Limitless Clients—Mindset & Foundations 1

    Chapter 1: Unshakeable Confidence 3

    Chapter 2: Organized Power - Conquer Chaos in Just 2 Hours a Day 15

    Chapter 3: Starting Strong - Get Clients Early 29

    Chapter 4: Time Mastery - Balance, Burnout-Proofing & Building Like a Boss 41

Section II: Prospecting & Conversion—Client Acquisition Magic 51

    Chapter 5: Breaking Barriers To Overcome Client Hurdles 53

    Chapter 6: Sell By Chat - DM Your Way to Booked Calls 63

    Chapter 7: Executive Targeting To Reach C-Level Clients & Build Coaching Funnels 85

    Chapter 8: The First Close - 7 Steps to Zoom Call Glory 91

Section III: Sealing the Deal & Scaling Up............... 109

    Chapter 9: Premium Enrollment - Command Top
        Dollar & Own the Money Talk.................. 111

    Chapter 10: Fulfillment Magic - Wow Your Clients
        and Keep Them Hooked 131

    Chapter 11: Automate, Win Corporates,
        Perfect Delivery............................... 147

    Chapter 12: Scaling to 100K/Month - Content,
        Delegation, and Cohort Mixology............... 161

Conclusion: Do the Opposite—Wisdom from Nightingale
    & Costanza...................................... 173

Acknowledgement..................................... 177

About The Author..................................... 179

INTRODUCTION

How to Get Clients, Make Bank, and Still Have a Life

"An entrepreneur is someone who will jump off a cliff and assemble an airplane on the way down."
– Reid Hoffman

Welcome to the Danger Zone. Let's face it—every genius is just a touch crazy. Not the padded-room kind, but the *good* kind of crazy. The kind that stands on the edge of a cliff takes a deep breath and swan-dives off like an unhinged mad scientist armed with duct tape and sheer audacity, frantically building a plane mid-freefall. And nope, no backup wingsuit—because that's for people who *plan* instead of *act*.

The entrepreneurial journey is bold, chaotic, and gloriously unpredictable—a high-stakes adventure where the fearless thrive. That's why the original cover of this book features an antique fighter plane blueprint, a timeless symbol of ingenuity and precision. Because building a business isn't just daring—it's a rocket-fueled, hair-on-fire kind of wild ride. While others scramble to stitch together parachutes mid-fall, I didn't just build a plane—I engineered a *7-Figure Formula* designed to cut through turbulence like Maverick blazing past the sound barrier on full afterburners. Buckle up.

This isn't some boring "How-To" guide. It's a turbocharged Danger Zone map for the bold and the brave. Why a Spitfire fighter plane? Because even in a world of AI and drones, humans still own the cockpit—observing, orienting, deciding, *acting*—the Maverick. And yeah, at mid-forties, I *am* Tom Cruise in *Top Gun*—old-school grit fused with new-school tools, still buzzing the tower just because I can.

But here's the deal: while the world's gone all-in on autopilot, this book is about flipping those switches *off*. Tech might crunch numbers, but it can't match the raw guts it takes to seize the moment, take the lead, and break formation when it counts. In a dogfight—or a sales call—it's still human instinct that beats every supercomputer on the planet. And this book? It's your flight school. I'll take your raw talent, hone it like a jet engine, and turn you into the ace of your industry—a conversation-creating machine that leaves your competitors sputtering on the runway.

Why This Matters

Four hundred million small businesses exist worldwide for a reason: people are done being told they're "Goose" when they know they're Maverick. They're sick of the grind, done with taking orders, and over letting someone else call the shots. It's time to break free, buzz the tower, and take control—because building wealth on your terms beats punching someone else's clock any day.

But let's be real—going solo isn't all barrel rolls and afterburners. You'll have to dodge doubters faster than a MiG at Mach 2 and survive the grilling of a drill instructor barking, "Do you even *belong* in this cockpit?" right before ordering you to do push ups until you're questioning every life choice that got you here.

That's why this book exists. It's not fluff, hype, or some wannabe wingman's pep talk. It's a battle-tested playbook to help you take the controls and build your dream life *now*—not in some "one-day" fantasy.

Steve Chandler said it best: *"Your bank account directly reflects your level of SERVICE."* And here's the truth that'll hit you harder than a G-force pull: only 5% of coaches hit seven figures, and less than 1% crack $1.5 million. I didn't just make it into that club—I flew in, flipped on the afterburners, and left vapor trails, not with cheap hacks or TikTok motivational memes, but by redefining what it means to be elite in a sky crowded with "just okay" coaches.

Let's Be Real

If you're chasing passive income fantasies, this book will feel like realizing your autopilot's broken mid-dogfight. "Set it and forget it" isn't a business plan; it's ejecting before takeoff. This journey is about grit, sweat, and mastering the moves that make clients *need* to work with you.

You know the line: "I feel the need—the need for speed!" That's the mindset. Two hours a day of fanatical prospecting—every single day—is all it takes to go from dreaming in the hangar to flying above the clouds.

So, if you're ready to ditch the excuses, grab the controls, and leave the doubters choking on your jet wash, let's get started. This isn't just about winning—it's about becoming the Top Gun of your industry. The stakes are high; the tower's given us clearance, and it's time to light the fires and kick the tires.

And if you're wondering whether I've got the credentials to back it up, let me drop this nugget on you: I've personally shared the stage with Kenny Loggins. Yes, *that* Kenny Loggins. Truth is stranger than fiction, my friend. But if I can survive the *actual* Danger Zone, I promise you're in good hands. Let's fly.

The Unlikely Birth of a Million-Dollar Coach

My first client? None other than a Mark Wahlberg venture. At 40, I dove headfirst into the coaching game. First few months? Brutal. After four months and countless hours, I'd scraped together a measly $9K. It was grind mode on steroids, and I was questioning everything. Then, my friend Lui from Down Under hit me with some Aussie-flavored reality: "You'll make millions doing this." Sounded nuts. Fast-forward five years, and I'm among the top 1% of coaches worldwide. How? Not by fairy dust but by transforming my mindset and 10X action that rewired my reality.

Ready to see what's possible?

Turn Your Life into a Cheat Code

Think of this manual as a time machine. It's the warp zone in Super Mario—the one that lets you skip the dead-end levels. Terrified to go solo? This book erases the terror. It's a no-BS playbook that brings in $150K+ a month. Imposter syndrome? Swipe left. Get ready to start raking in $5-10K per month while half-asleep.

Picture this: the average American makes $55K a year. You? Achieving that in a few weeks. No boss, no commute, no wasted energy. Remember those hidden tunnels and infinite lives in Mario? That's what this is. Not just a book, but your VIP access to the back door of business success—a whole new game.

Unlimited lives? Yep. Infinite money glitch? Right here. This book isn't just another bestseller; it's about to be the most dog-eared, highlighted, "Can you believe it's that simple?" guide on your shelf. Let's do this!

Is this you? You love coaching and consulting, but you're struggling with one, some or all of the following common challenges:

- Gurus bark, "Find a niche!" while you're like, "Find me a nap." Even Steve Chandler, coaching's Godfather, says, "Niche rhymes with quiche, and both should stay in France."

- Coaching's supposed to be the dream, but you're stuck at $5K/month, which feels like working hard to stay broke.

- You stare at the ceiling every night, whispering, "Why does nobody want this?" like you're summoning ghosts of failed launches.

- Every book or course you buy is just overpriced fluff, plus a free side hustle as someone else's unpaid consultant.

- Everyone and their dog is now a "coach" or "GTM advisor," and you're convinced you need a Nobel Prize or a TED Talk to compete.

- Your emotions rotate between impostor syndrome, writer's block, and perfectionism—a mental three-ring circus with no audience.

Is this you? In your heart of hearts, you want so badly to achieve one, some, or all of the following dream outcomes:

Clients are lining up to work with you like you're the only bartender at happy hour.

- You're serving up business breakthroughs like a Michelin-star chef, and your clients can't get enough of the secret sauce.

- You've ditched your 9-5 like a bad one-night stand and are living it up—working part-time from anywhere, making $500-$2,000 an hour for sharing your brilliance with people who actually *get* you.

- You're smashing through your income ceiling like a Miley Cyrus wrecking ball, hitting $100K+ months, and setting up camp in the land of "FU Money."

- Your client acquisition system is so slick it could sell ice to penguins—energizing, effective, and leaving prospects thanking *you* for showing up.

- You're living the dream, jet-setting like a travel influencer, and flipping the rat race the bird from your spot in the lap of luxury.

If you want all this and more, you're in luck: Writing this, I'm sitting in Zurich after stints living in Dubai, Italy, and hopping around Europe, catching some tunes at the Montreux Jazz Festival and taking in the art at *La Biennale di Venezia*.

Life doesn't suck, and it wasn't that long ago that I was nose-to-the-grind-stone, stressed out of my mind as a VP of Sales in SaaS, trading my health and happiness for what I now know better as a fraction of my potential - even at a $200,000 base salary (no company will EVER value you at your true worth - it's simple economics). I'm blessed to say that's a month's work for me now. I'll show you how to do it all if you follow my advice.

This is my power user manual, or *7-Figure Formula*, which lays out precisely the *JMM™ 3 Walls Model*, a framework for advanced client acquisition. My secrets have helped me do 100K, 200K, and 300K months, and it will work like clockwork for coaches, consultants, speakers, advisors, fractionals, side hustlers, and solopreneurs. More importantly, clients like Scott Martinis have gone from 5K/mo to 35K/mo in 6 weeks. You can breathe easy knowing none of the standard guru playbooks will be deployed here:

- No websites that scream "K-Mart Tony Robbins" with a side of budget inspirational quotes.
- No ads or click funnels straight out of the Alex Hormozi Hustle Factory.
- No cold calling like you're auditioning for *Grant Cardone's 10X Telethon:* "No interest? That's a *type* of interest!"
- No ruining your dinner with cringey selfie videos while your pasta gets cold.
- No niching yourself into a corner, no impossible guarantees, and absolutely no refunds. My time is $500-$2K/hr—just like a top attorney. I guarantee *me,* not miracles.
- No MLM-style "certifications" that do nothing except confirm you're a "certified" sucker.

None of these goofy tropes work. What does? Creating a robust frame by leveraging advanced *JMM*™ formulas and breaking through the *3 Walls*. Unlike the carnival barkers using passive inbound "marketing" hacks on the rubes in the audience, we execute outbound like professionals: calm, cool, and collected. They'll never see you coming!

The 3 Walls

1 Nobody wants it

Stage 1 Connect / Invite
via DMs & 4th Frame

Stage 2 Enroll
via Zoom

Stage 3 Offer
Fees

2 Nobody has any money

Stage 4 Breakthrough
Investing in you

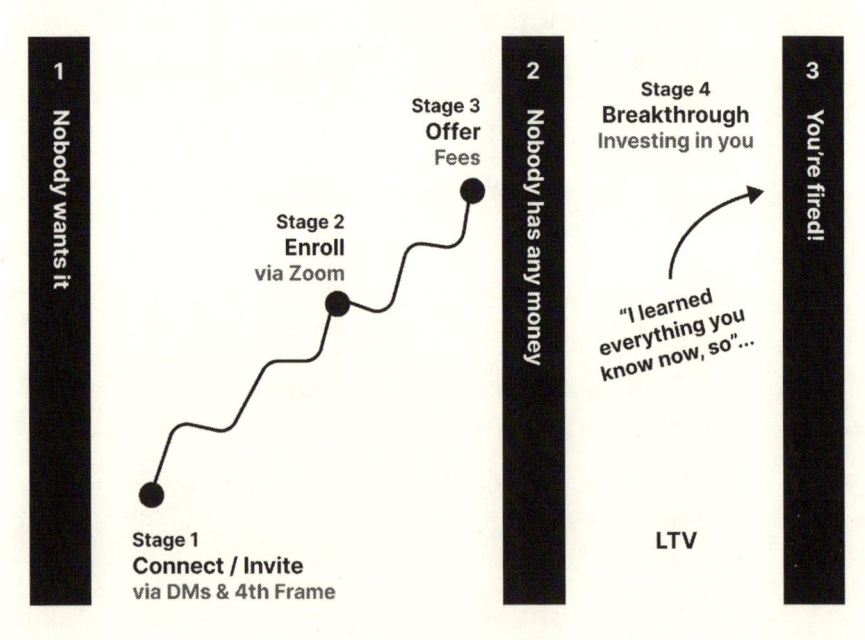

"I learned everything you know now, so"...

LTV

3 You're fired!

Phil Smith Design

This book is the golden goose if you are a coach, consultant, advisor, speaker, fractional, side hustler, or solopreneur. I'm living proof that its contents can and *will* make you millions.

The final exam for my elite clients is to master client acquisition to such a degree that we could put you in the witness protection program, change your name, and drop you off in Milwaukee, Wisconsin ("Undercover Coach" coming to a streaming service near you!). Within six months, you'd earn $250K/yr with your eyes closed, applying these simple, counter-intuitive techniques.

Coaching is not about your CV, MBA, how many exits you have, or any other vanity metrics. It's a game of reverse psychology and relationship dynamics, and it's always and *only* based on the actual results your potential clients believe you can bring to them, based on how you've served others who will advocate for you.

We live in the AI revolution, a topic I covered in *JMM 2.0*, but the methods of *4.0* exist separately from "the rise of the machines." Being an agent of change requires beating the bots by being "more human than a human" and practicing active listening while demonstrating acumen, insight, and empathy—traits inherently creating a polarity shift. As Dale Carnegie once said, "To be interesting, be interested."

The only greater mystery than "how do I get unlimited clients" is "how do I create a breakthrough on every first call?" Once I cracked this, I emotionally closed 100% of clients (Step 1). With their buy-in secured, helping them from the same side of the table makes finding the money a logical last step.

What do I mean by this? Every close happens in two acts: The "emotional close" when you know their heart is in it, and "finding the money" as the final consummation. Once you have the emotional commitment, it's time to start earning your title as a trusted advisor – previously unidentified stakeholders will emerge from the woodwork to help you get the deal done.

"This sounds great, but I gotta talk to my wife," your fledgling client interjects. What better way to show them how to navigate challenging conversations than inviting her to your next call? Without support at home, your work together is cooked right out of the gate, so you better secure buy-in. You'll find that tackling this head-on will earn you respect, with the additional benefit that partners, siblings, and business partners will ALSO turn into clients. Lemons into lemonade. Lesson #118 *JMM*!

A note from a mentor, the living legend Charles H. Green, who co-wrote *The Trusted Advisor:*

"My first 20 years of consulting taught me that problem definition is about 10X more valuable than problem solution. It ensures you're solving the right problem. It took me 20 years of consulting to learn that a shared problem definition is about 20 times more valuable than successfully defining it independently.

Solo problem definition is an exercise in mental masturbation. Rarely have I seen a client de novo convinced of a problem definition solely by my brilliant exposition. Have I seen a client buy a definition/solution that doesn't link to some deeply held viewpoint, value, or belief that the client already has?

The conclusion: from the first interaction, sit on the same side of the metaphorical table. Mutually admit ignorance and commit to a genuinely collaborative search for the correct problem definition; skip all the credentialing and demonstrations of your experience and intellect, roll up your sleeves, and work with your new partner-in-training. The rest takes care of itself."

The coaching industry is growing alarmingly, but only among the top 1% of prospects with resources. For the 99%, coaching has fallen on the priority list. It's a sad state of global affairs, but you're not reading this book to storm the White House; you're looking to maximize your earnings immediately.

Once you've mastered the essentials, go deep into the writings of Alan Weiss and David C. Baker, who do $5MM+ per year *solo*. I've studied them both and deconstructed their playbooks into "first principles" to put my unique spin on how all coaches can land high-fee clients.

Everybody else hits around 1MM top line and kills their cash flow with low ticket courses, staffing up with full-time equivalents (FTEs), and delegation. You won't. I'll teach you to earn $500-2K/hr *solo* by talking, 100% pure profit. Nobody wants to hire Justin Michael and hear, "Great, here's my sub-trainer Phil. He's certified on *JMM*." No!

They want the real McCoy, YOU!

SECTION I

Limitless Clients– Mindset & Foundations

"Become a millionaire not for the million dollars, but for what it will make of you to achieve it."

– Jim Rohn

CHAPTER 1

Unshakeable Confidence

"What's the secret to a great coaching practice? Great clients."

– Steve Chandler

Welcome to the laboratory of a human alchemist. My life? It's delightfully absurd. Each day, I wake up, meet remarkable people, turn their world on its head, and walk away with fees that would make most people's jaws drop. They take that transformation, amplify it, and watch as double-digit returns ripple through their lives—and the lives they touch. I've turned the daily grind into a high-stakes, high-impact, virtuous cycle that's as profitable as it is powerful. But let's get one thing straight—it wasn't always this way. I didn't stumble into this world. I built it. And you're about to find out *how*.

I distinctly recall couch surfing in my mid-twenties and trying to convince a startup company to raise my $800/mo pay to $2,500 if I worked 60 hours a week. My innate gifts and talents lay dormant, and unlike the wunderkinds gracing Forbes' *30 under 30,* I was a late bloomer when it came to earning money. Once I cracked it, I realized it was far easier than I thought.

The blunt truth is that it's easier to make seven figures solo than grind it out in middle management at some faceless corporation.

Reread that and shout it out loud for the cheap seats in the back. Take heed if you're in the nosebleeds now because I see a skybox in your future.

What is this mysterious craft passed down called "coaching" or "consulting?"

The truth is alchemical: *Turning human potential into gold.*

So, if you're reading this, it's a great honor and massive responsibility to come through for you. This is the hardest-hitting, badass, and most potent guide laden with every last secret to how I built everything.

The trick to this business is that you have to love doing it. You must fall in love with every aspect of the process, not just the coaching delivery and fulfillment side but especially the lost art of net new client acquisition.

Especially *prospecting*—don't even call it that anymore. Think of it as "talking to quality humans" or simply "talking to people all day." In the same way, we've redefined closing as "enrolling." Those old terms carry too much baggage—pain, rejection, and drudgery. Instead, start each day with an open heart and mind, ready to chop wood and carry water.

To build a full, thriving practice, you may initially spend up to 80% of your time prospecting—so it's essential to reframe it as something you genuinely enjoy. Cultivating this mindset fuels the stamina you need to persevere. Remember, it's a marathon, not a sprint until you secure those first 5 to 15 clients.

Don't let negativity wear you down. Many people—colleagues, competitors, and even strangers—will respond with jealousy, bitterness, and even hostility. Let it slide. You're interrupting people, after all; any seasoned cold caller understands this. It's part of the job, part of the journey.

Any amateur can "coach" their buddies or their buddies' buddies, but it takes a true professional to go out into the world and spread the gospel to total strangers.

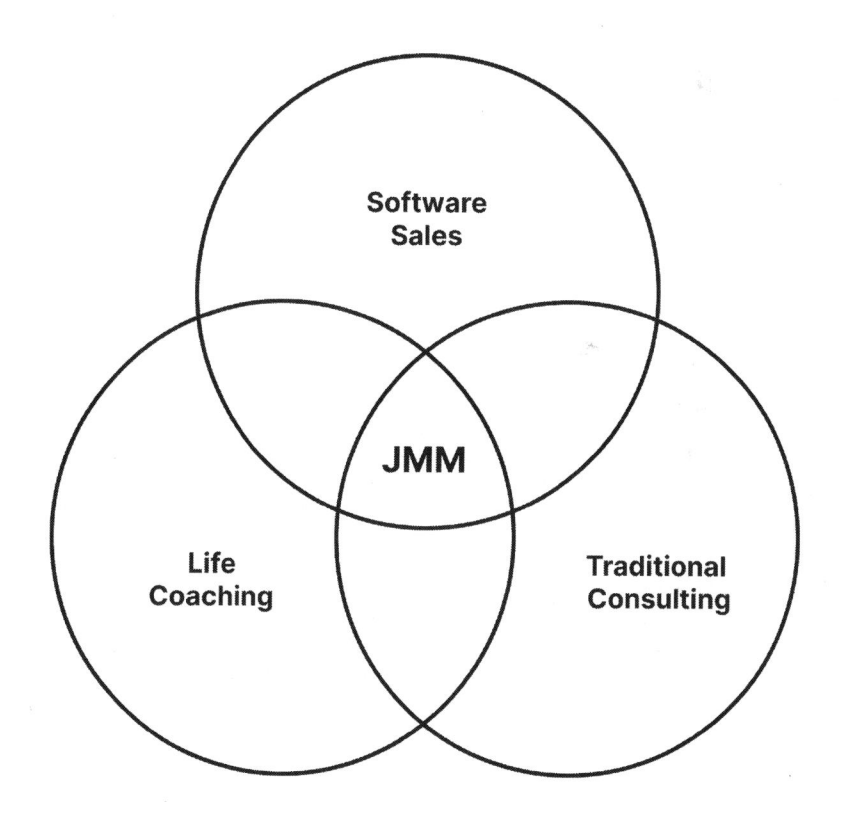

I have studied the methods of elite coaching practitioners worldwide from various disciplines and synthesized the learnings from hundreds of books so you don't have to. Most of the principles in this book are 1,000-year-old truths of human nature that will be relevant in another 1,000 years.

A Disclaimer: Many of these arts are counterintuitive, meaning your results may temporarily decrease as you develop your skills. It is critical to persevere: I've taken hundreds of clients through this process who stick with it and double, triple, or even quintuple their income.

Unlock Your Inner Superhero (Cape Optional)

Here's a secret weapon against self-doubt that works every time: grab a blank page and draw a timeline. Start with your birth date. Next, add your first steps into the workforce, your proudest professional moments, and any year you courageously endured an annual performance review. Watch your story unfold!

Now think about the people who chose you—those who hired you, invested in you, or at least didn't run the other way. This isn't just a timeline; it's proof that you've been conquering self-doubt since you figured out how to get dressed in the morning. Every step led you here; self-doubt is toast, and you've got the timeline to prove it.

If you have a job, congratulations! Two things are true: (1) You've got some skills, and (2) someone is actually paying you to use them. Moving into coaching or consulting is essentially leveling up your skills and pinpointing where you can really blow people's minds. That's why asking your closest 5 to 15 people about your "expertise" is so powerful, as David C. Baker points out in *The Business of Expertise*. It's a bit like having a superpower you didn't realize, except without the need for a cape (unless that's your style).

Another exercise? Get those testimonials and let them marinate. Let their validation spill over you in written form or video like the calmest, most reassuring tidal wave. Cut down on the negative self-talk. I outline a solid affirmation practice in *Attraction Selling (JMM 3.0)*, which works if you let it.

When I'm coaching coaches, consultants, advisors, or anyone else trying to break out of the imposter-syndrome rut, the biggest hurdle is the comparison game: "I didn't have five exits," they say, or "I wasn't the top rep at Oracle or Salesforce." Listen, clients don't care about your vanity metrics. They're not hiring you because of some impressive LinkedIn numbers; they're hiring you because you know something they don't. And if that isn't a power move, I don't know what is.

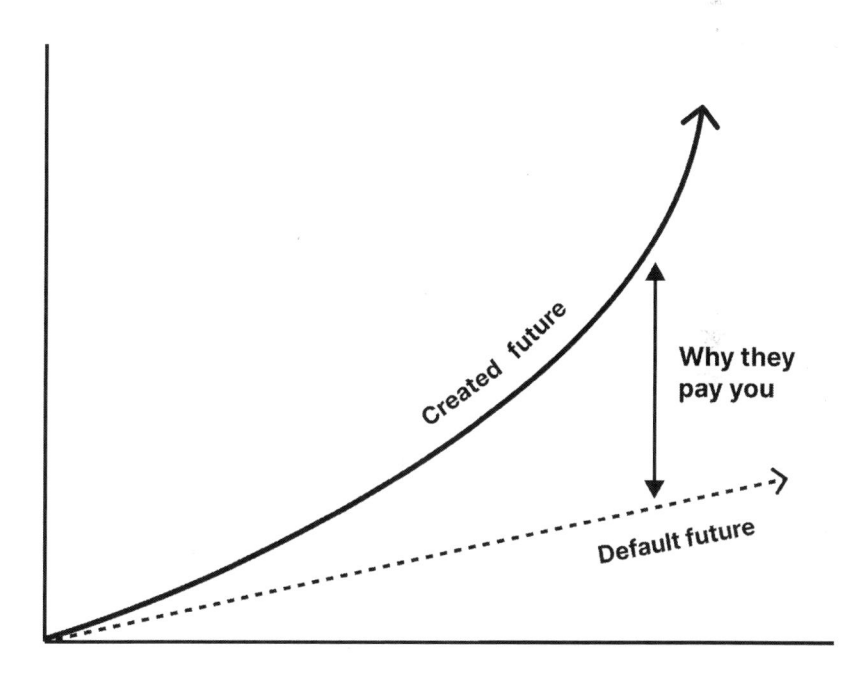

© *Steve Chandler & Rich Litvin*

What obstacles stand between your client and their dream—the ones you're here to help them overcome?

Your results are your calling card. If you're just starting your business, leverage the *First Circle* process from Steve Chandler and Rich Litvin to get initial testimonials and case studies *from people you already know* that you can promote and leverage to get the flywheel of client acquisition turning. My clients are always my best salespeople and referral sources.

You must drive testimonials and social proof from the beginning of the 3-Wall JMM Model.

If nothing in this book works for you, the problem is probably your testimonials—they lack punch. People want results they can see, hear, and measure. Start small if you have to: free or low-fee clients can give you the jaw-dropping success stories you need to charge big bucks.

Whether you're a mindset coach, conflict whisperer, manifestation wizard, or one of 31 other flavors of guru, remember: people pay big for proof. Make your testimonials scream results, and your clients will sell you better than you ever could.

"Don't take my word for it; talk to my clients." (bold solution to everything!)

Just trust me here: skipping this step has led to clients struggling for many more months than needed. If you have the bedrock of raving clients, you'll create unshakeable champions pushing through the direct messages (DMs), the discovery call, into the negotiation, and close. Clients who feel your self-belief and extreme belief in *them* will see an ROI.

Any ambivalence or wishy-washiness here, and they just won't be able to trust you enough to pay you. That's the chronic "I need to think about it" or when the client tells me, "Every prospect is just wasting my time; I'm not targeting the right people." 3% of people can not only afford your fee but are in the buying window; you're just not confident *you* can help them. Sales is the transference of belief.

"How are you different?" "Talk to my clients." You can't self-reference; success relies on what your clients say. If you're side hustling, build testimonials to get people to vouch for you: "Justin drove X results over Y timeline." If clients have to "think it over," they're stuck in fear and doubt. Our job as enrollers is to inject them with certainty in our ability to help them as we've helped others. I'm hammering this point because it's the #1 reason you'll get clients from this book.

If you do this wrong, you'll lose clients who are more prosperous than you are, and imposter syndrome will rear its ugly head. Rich Litvin coaches Olympians, millionaires, and billionaires. I've finally started working with some B2B celebrities, and it's a gas. Remember, if you have an advanced skill set to impart, they universally need you!

We all have the same hopes, fears, quirks, and dreams. These high-end, "untouchable" elite clients you hesitate to contact are often the best to coach, have no pressure on paying your fee, and have a growth mindset that has already got them to where they are today. The clients you fear are often the best match. "Feel the fear and do it anyway!" (Jack Canfield)

Finding Great Clients & The Two Closes

As I mentioned, every coaching call has two moments of truth: The "emotional close" and the "money close." People love to *buy* but hate to be *sold*. My secret sauce? I get clients so emotionally invested they're practically lighting candles in my honor. They see value, hear angels sing, and feel an undeniable urge to work with me. It's like a primal need, somewhere between a crush and a revelation.

Then we dive into "finding the money" – it's like a treasure hunt with more drama. My clients have sold Bitcoin, cashed out Google stock, hit up Grandma for a "loan," and occasionally considered the organ market. But hey, with my 97% success rate, I sleep just fine; the ROI comes back 5-15 fold. So, let them dig a little—it's character-building. Sometimes, a random Great Aunt they've never heard of swoops in, and boom, transformation funded!

Now, who are the best clients to close? It's a trick question: Only the ones who can pay, of course! Look, if 60-80% of reps miss quota, as every sales survey ever confirms, they're likely coasting on base salary. So, if you're a rep reading this, learn from my 15-year journey—don't wait forever to get that high-performing side hustle going.

And if you're targeting reps, remember: all that glitters isn't OTE (On-Target Earnings). Forget the RepVue comp reports—many reps are just base-lining it. That's why you get creative. Think outside the box: savings, investments, brokerage accounts, crypto, family members they forgot about, maybe even a good ol' yard sale.

Targeting is an art. Think about the newbie business development rep (BDR) leader who just got promoted vs. the seasoned VP vs. the non-existent leader (no, that's not a typo; those are real). Think about their years in the game, the company's health, and the mysterious 1% with that hidden "X-factor"—family money, a lucky stock win, or maybe they just know how to work it.

Troubleshooting: My clients need help with target clarity, often ruminating over their niche and ideal client profile (ICP).

They obsess over questions like, "Should I coach CEOs or Founders?" or "Should I offer growth advisory, go-to-market (GTM) strategy, or sales training?"

Realize that you can coach *any* client. Work with people who appreciate you and can afford your fee. It's crazy simple.

1. Do they respect you? (aka, there's a mutual interest, just like in dating)
2. Can you do something better than they can? (competency transfer)
3. Can they afford your fee? (somehow)

Run your business borderless, "let your fingers do the walking." On any given day, I'll be coaching from Singapore to Australia, the EU, and Canada. I grew like gremlins outside the US in the first few years as it was a blue ocean compared to the red ocean of 10,000 American trainers and every side-hustling rep with a newsletter cloning my Codices (cheat-code guides).

You don't need to close everyone! If they are super nitpicky and run an Oren Klaff "analyst frame" where they question everything, just walk away.

Gifts vs. Talents—Unlocking Your True Strengths

Your gifts are like superpowers—so natural you don't notice them. But talents? Different story. Those demand sweat, resilience, and enough practice hours to make Beethoven look lazy. But here's the cheat code to absolute mastery: it's not about grinding till you're miserable. Absolute mastery (and becoming an elite coach or consultant) is cranking up your gifts to 11. Yes, this is your *Spinal Tap* moment! When you dial up what makes you "you," you're not just chasing greatness—you're living it, rock star style.

Talents / Gifts

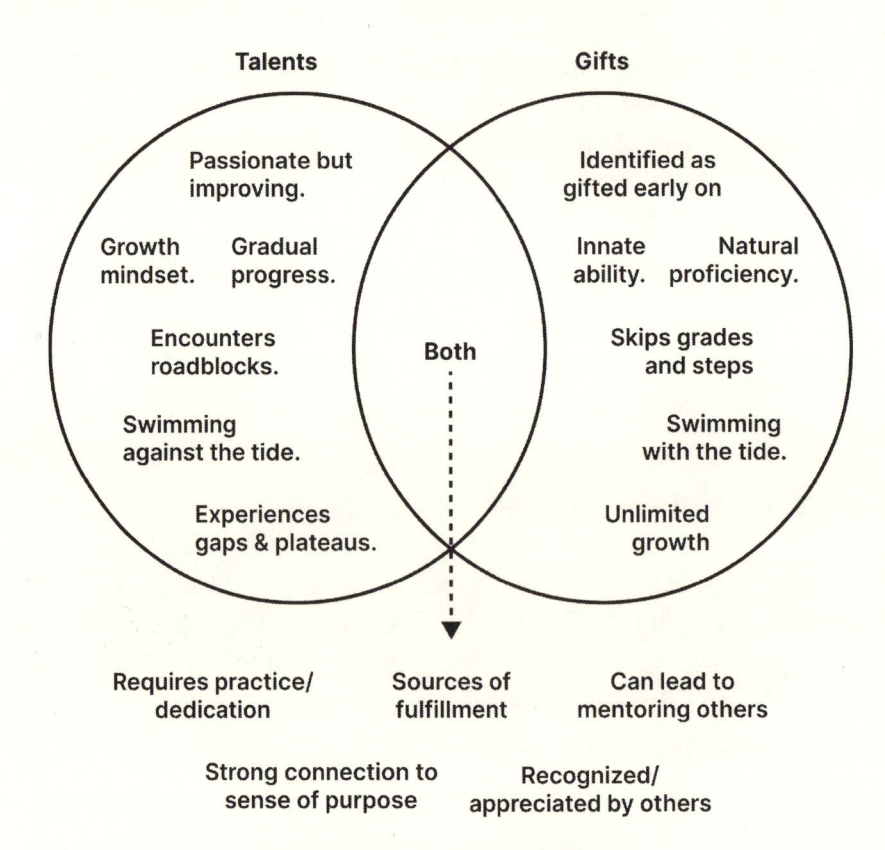

Talents:
- Passionate but improving.
- Growth mindset.
- Gradual progress.
- Encounters roadblocks.
- Swimming against the tide.
- Experiences gaps & plateaus.

Gifts:
- Identified as gifted early on
- Innate ability.
- Natural proficiency.
- Skips grades and steps
- Swimming with the tide.
- Unlimited growth

Both:
- Requires practice/dedication
- Sources of fulfillment
- Can lead to mentoring others
- Strong connection to sense of purpose
- Recognized/appreciated by others

Image by Shannon Needham

By age 10, my teacher told me I was the best writer she'd seen in 30 years. I shrugged it off until I hit 40. The first time I wrote a book pitch? Landed a deal with a fat advance from a top-five publisher. Procrastination level: expert.

"Give me a lever long enough and a fulcrum to place it, and I shall move the world." – Archimedes (translation: if you find your genius zone, it's game over.)

Grab a Venn Diagram and do some detective work on your greatest gift. Once you nail that unique zone of genius, dive in. Forget

80/20—that's playing it safe. Go 99/1, like Richard Koch's *Star Principle*: the top 1% of actions that drive 99% of results. That's how he scored big with Betfair and retired with a fortune. (Note: to retire with millions, you must start with...millions. But you get the idea.)

As for me? My *Star Principle* moves are simple: I write, read, coach, and talk for a living. That's it. I'm double-dipping into what I was born to do, and let me tell you, the results have been chef's kiss spectacular.

> ***"The power of a brand is inversely proportional to its scope."***
>
> *— Al Ries*

> ***"Losers spray, winners focus."***
>
> *— Steve Chandler*

Thrive-First Success - The Ankush Jain Model for Momentum

Imagine this: instead of the usual sales song and dance that feels like emotional dodgeball, you pull a total 180. Inspired by Ankush Jain's *Sweet Sharing*, you hand your clients the keys from day one—like a driving instructor who genuinely believes they won't plow into a mailbox. Your mantra? "Thrive First." The twist? You give them the VIP experience before they've even forked over a dime. You're not just buttering them up; you're practically air-dropping confidence and letting them know they're *already* set to make it rain on your coaching.

Forget the tired old tactics: no endless upsells, no click funnels lurking around every corner, no suspiciously cheap $97 "limited-time offers" meant to leave them wanting more. Transformation is the appetizer, main course, and dessert in your world. By the time you reach commitment, they're already sold—not because you twisted their arm, but because they know you're the real deal. This isn't just coaching; it's coaching with the volume on 11.

Kill off the profit motive.

Forget profit. Who needs it? I give away 99% of my content for free and open source so that the other 1% will boomerang back and hire me anyway. It's like a karmic sales funnel—whenever I give more, people in my inbox ask, "Can I pay you now?" I work like Rocky, training Creed with clients I believe in, helping them go from zero to hero, and primed to invest in the full *JMM* experience.

Mastering *JMM* isn't just reading a manual; it's like earning a third-degree black belt. You can memorize every page, every kata, but it's all theory until you're on the mat, sweating and bruised. Don't worry, though. Ninety days on this program, and you'll be a revenue assassin—like Steven Seagal, but with better aim and a cooler ponytail. You'll be flipping polarity, closing deals, and fishing Zoom calls out of LinkedIn like a grizzly bear swiping salmon in Alaska. Hopefully, your politics are *a hair* more dialed in.

> *"Give away the secrets, sell the implementation."*
> — *Alex Hormozi*

The secret is this: zero expectations, zero resentment. Give with an open heart, like Bob Burg preaches in *The Go-Giver*. Pour into people, believe in them, and watch them soar. Sometimes, all anyone needs is a little faith and a nudge to break through.

> *"Your income is determined by how many people you serve and how well you serve them."*
> — *Bob Burg*

CHAPTER 2

Organized Power - Conquer Chaos in Just 2 Hours a Day

"Be independent of the good opinion of other people."

– Abraham Maslow

Picture this: I'm talking to thousands of people at once, and no, I haven't cloned myself (yet). My secret weapon? One legendary spreadsheet—a single, powerhouse list of thousands, all united by one thing: *intent*. These aren't just random names; they've raised their hands, waved their flags, or at least given a casual nod that says, "I want to work with you."

This isn't just a list; it's Ari Gold's dream roster without the chair-throwing or profanity that could scorch a script. One glance, one message, and bam—you're channeling that "hug it out" energy into landing your next Aquaman deal with James Cameron—no tantrum required.

I constantly stack rank and color code that list to track down the warmer leads with the stealth of a honey badger in business attire. But I don't just hit them with a "Hey, wanna buy?" I come with flair and finesse: video drops, memes, diagrams, articles, PDFs, guides, Substack updates, and custom YouTube videos. This list? It's like a pet Venus flytrap that grows bigger every time you feed it, and it's hungry for ideas, content, and some personality. "Feed me, Seymour!" You're running a media empire of one: YOU NEWS NETWORK!

Let's talk about LinkedIn's Inbox—a screaming inferno of "Hi, let's connect!" that makes your email inbox look like a soothing day at the spa. You can "star" essential chats, like handing out kindergarten gold stars, but let's be honest—when every message is yelling "ASAP," those stars feel about as effective as a paper umbrella in a hurricane.

Enter AI tools, the Marie Kondo of LinkedIn, here to sort the chaos with robotic precision, quietly asking, "Does this generic pitch spark joy?" (Spoiler: No. But nuking it into oblivion? Oh, that's the good stuff.)

Give, give, give—and then give some more until people say, "Okay, okay, I get it!"

Eventually, your future clients bubble up like a hot tub time machine from all the value you're pouring in. And WhatsApp? It's like the bat signal for personal connections. You can build private groups, DM until your thumbs hurt, and drop voice notes like the 7-figure coaches. Why voice notes? Because nothing says "I'm real" like hearing someone's voice. Stephen Covey calls it "speed to trust." I call it "voice notes: the secret weapon you didn't know you needed." Any given day, I've had over a dozen live conversations while you're still fussing with your AI personalization widget du jour.

Think Omnichannel

LinkedIn isn't about sending one magic message and riding off into the sunset like some prospecting Wyatt Earp. Nope, it's more like trying to open a stubborn jar of pickles—it takes 3 to 5 firm twists (aka touches) before you hear the satisfying pop of a response. Persistence and creativity are your power tools. LinkedIn is also the higher-status playground for starting a prospecting workflow. Just don't be the person throwing sand in everyone's face.

Ironically, if you train teams on phone skills but start cold-calling willy-nilly, prospects might think, "Wait, if this guy's a top trainer, how does he have time to call little ol' me? Shouldn't he be flying private or something?" That's why cold calling works better as a down-funnel move. Once you've exchanged a few messages on LinkedIn or WhatsApp, calling out of the blue makes sense. Just make it seem like you're squeezing them between high-powered meetings or dodging paparazzi. A quick, breezy voice note or call can cement your high-status frame. You're not just talking the talk; you're walking the "I drink my own champagne" walk.

Boldness is the secret sauce to landing clients. Be willing to ruffle feathers, polarize, and—gasp—be disliked. People don't follow beige, vanilla leaders who are too afraid to say anything controversial. They follow bold, opinionated badasses like Winston Churchill. You know, the guy who unabashedly said, "Let's never surrender... and also pass me another cigar." Run your business like a high school popularity contest, and sure, everyone might like you—but your bank account will look like it just graduated with a degree in basket weaving. The greats? They've got more haters than in *Mean Girls*. Constantly. It's practically a KPI.

And let's talk perception versus reality: looking *too* available is like wearing sweatpants to a black-tie event if you're a consultant. Scarcity creates value. Consider McKinsey—mystique, prestige, and a whiff of "You're lucky we even took your call" allows them to charge *yuge* hourly rates. You'd never hear them say, "Hey, I'm free all next week; what works for you?" (Insert laugh track here.) So, even if you're just starting, fake it 'til you make it; pretend your calendar is already bursting at the seams. That confidence? It's magnetic.

Here's the ultimate client hack: Get their WhatsApp or text. Real-time chats = faster deals. It's like turning your business into a speed-dating champ—except everyone swipes right!

When deals close, it's wild. "There's never a 'No,' just a *not yet*." Legendary coaches like Litvin and Chandler echo this sentiment, which is so true. I'll close a client and look at my list, and it's #986. They boomerang back after 6-18 months, even 2+ years of nurture. I call this "The Boomerang Effect!"

Commit to this business long-term. Play the long game.

Take the 'L' with Style and a Smile

That's why embracing your client when they reject you is so important. Treat them like gold—sparkly, shiny, 24-karat Bruno Mars gold. They'll remember that and, more importantly, notice the absence of commission breath. (That sour desperation sellers reek of, like they'd trade dignity for sneakers. It's the Axe Body Spray of sales—100% effective at repelling.) Instead, leave them with a fresh, minty impression. One that makes them think, "Wow, they're not just trying to sell me... they might be human."

When humans want something life-changing, they'll sell a kidney or dig deep in the couch cushions for spare change.

If you get overbooked (and you should because you're awesome), don't panic! Make a waitlist. Book out in advance. Raise your fees like Beyoncé announces tour dates—calm, confident, and unapologetic. I don't block my evenings and weekends only to try and solve Sudoku puzzles or practice my best Jason Statham impression in the mirror (confession: I'm nailing it), BUT because it gives me wiggle room. If my diary needs a quick shuffle, I'm ready. Remember: it's not a race to charge the most; it's about giving the best value. Think of yourself as the Michelin-starred restaurant of your industry—exclusive, high quality, and worth the splurge.

The 2-Hour Rule–Relentless Prospecting Discipline

Here's the deal: if your business isn't bursting at the seams with clients, you should prospect like it's an Olympic sport—80% of the time, no excuses.

If you don't have 2 hours a day to go full-on "honey badger," Steven Brady even put together a Notion doc for my 55-minute LinkedIn Workout adapted from *JMM 1.0: Sales Superpowers*. Every coach has to hustle for themselves, so I dedicated a whole chapter to this art of the hunt.

I've talked to the heavyweights in this game. Sure, they'll have the occasional VA, SDR, or appointment setter (and believe me, I've tried them all—from Denmark to Delhi). But here's the kicker: top earners like Rich Habets, Ankush Jain, Carolyn Freyer-Jones, Steve Hardison, Melissa Ford, Karen Davis, Townsend Wardlaw, and Scott Leese know that real magic happens when they're the ones reaching out—no bots, no recycled scripts—just raw, human-to-human connection, like the troglodytes of high-ticket sales.

Here's how to nail my 2-hour daily prospecting routine *and* have fun doing it:

- **Block out two 45-minute sessions:** You can't "Always Be Prospecting" (ABP) if you're "Always Being Distracted." Treat this time like it's sacred—if Mark Cuban called, you'd tell him, "Sorry, I'm prospecting."

- **Fix your LinkedIn feed:** Hit "follow" 200+ times on perfect targets like Black Friday. When you're done, your feed will be rich with leads instead of your cousin's vacation photos. (VPs and CXOs with 7+ years' experience scream "$3K+/mo client," so focus there.)

- **Use tools for a curated feed:** AI-powered automation and analytics turn your feed into a magic show—poof, prospects appear out of nowhere! Sales Nav tries, but it's more like sawing yourself in half—effective, sure, but who has the energy?

- **Only talk to people you like.** Yogi Berra's wisdom is, "Only close clients who can afford your fee." Translation? There are no window shoppers, no "I'll think about it" types, and no one whose profile screams "still splitting Wi-Fi with the neighbors."

- **Put on a vibe soundtrack:** Sacred frequencies like 432 Hz or 528 Hz are excellent for spiritual and financial alignment. Not your thing? Go for Taylor Swift, a podcast, or whatever gets you hyped to close deals.

- **Stop being a perfectionist:** Just show up and DM people. Use *The 4th Frame*™ and *7-Step Close Process*™ like a Swiss Army knife—it doesn't matter if you don't know all the functions; just start cutting. Remember Guy Kawasaki's advice: "Don't worry, be crappy."

- **Get chatty with a 2:1 ratio:** They should reply twice for every message you send. How? Ask provocative questions like:
  - "What's the biggest deal you've ever closed?"
  - "If you doubled your revenue tomorrow, what would break first?"
  - "What's stopping you from hiring someone amazing (hint: me)?"

- **"Fat stacks in the circle backs" – Ryan Reisert:** Follow up relentlessly but with charm. Email them a screenshot of their DM to jog their memory. Show proof like Sherlock solving a case for warm referrals: "Look! You said yes. Let's chat."

- **Make the bold ask:** After a great call, leave an assumptive voice note or DM like, "Ready to go, Kurt?" or "What's the good word?" Confidence shows leadership, and where you lead, they'll follow. Seal the deal with, "I'll send a simple invoice for $XK/mo. Once the transfer's done, we're good to go. It has credit and e-check options." They'll jump out of the plane like *The Flying Elvises* before you say, "Deal closed."

- **Pro Tip: Stalk smarter.** Nearly every LinkedIn first-degree connection has an email hidden under "Contact Info." Click it, grab it, and use it. Voilà—your omnichannel follow-up just got easier.

Now, crush those sessions and make it rain.

Hit them with a mix of video drops, voice notes, and the occasional GIF barrage—just enough to keep them guessing and you memorable. I've got a whole army of prospects who received 20+ messages from me with crickets in response. And yet, sometimes, message 21 is the tipping point. Persistence pays off, but only if you keep it spicy—like a plot twist in *Billions*, not *Gossip Girl*. Toss in a Venn diagram, a killer quote, or a case study. Keep them hooked like it's the finale, not a rerun.

Touch one: drop a cheeky "spark" one-liner. Touch two: follow up with a cat GIF (who can resist?). Touch three: share a use case that'll have them thinking, "Ouch, that's me." (*JMM 1.0* and *Codex 9-11* explain this in glorious detail.)

And yes, the top reply I get on LinkedIn is, "Are you a bot?" My response? "If I had a bot this smooth, I'd be a billionaire by now!"

Brian Burns said best: "What is not overtly positive is covertly negative." So, if you're getting ghosted on a cold thread, don't sweat it; it's static. But if they go MIA after a first call, that's a red flag. When that happens, throw a friendly nudge: "What's coming up for you since we last met?"

Or return to the last "hook point" (shoutout to Neil Strauss), where they got honest about their goals or limiting beliefs: "I was just thinking about your goal to hit seven figures. I have some thoughts on how to make it more achievable." GIF bumps are fun, but you've got to put some meat on that bone.

And here's my #1 tip: SLOW the F DOWN. Be the world's happiest garden snail.

Slow down, observe, and research. There are no more one-size-fits-all "spark" openers. Be human; think like your prospect. Dive into their recent activity, look for an opening, and add value where it matters.

Go wide on LinkedIn with plenty of "sparks" (light, witty, SMS-style messages to 1st-degree connections) and "spears" (sharp, social-proof-packed InMails for 2nd-degree connections). Think of it like Crocodile Dundee fishing with dynamite at the top of the funnel—100 a day? Perfectly fine. But the moment someone bites, kill your automation like it's a bad first date, take a deep breath, and start a real conversation. Ask them what they're aiming for, what drives them, what they've tried, and what's holding them back. Then, reel it in with a Zoom invite. Hook, line, and booked!

This "7-step" rhythm pops up all over this manual because, like gravity yanking an apple off a tree, the psychology of DMs is universal. Since cracking this formula, I've pulled thousands of chats onto Zoom—even with CROs who probably started the call wondering why they agreed to it in the first place.

And remember: GIFs are cute, but knowing when to send one? *That's* the actual art.

Look:

> *"Since working with Justin, my team has made a 180% increase in closed business (2.2MM) and a 300% increase in validated pipeline. He is, no doubt, the best of the best & all the rest. Great investment!"*
>
> *– Mark C. Green, CRO, Televox*

When chatting with people, don't just pitch like you're on *Shark Tank*—send them testimonials, blogs, podcast appearances, chapters from your book, or even that article you read at 2 a.m. while stress-eating Doritos. Go all-in and send a custom video that screams, "Look, I actually did my homework on you!" Give,

give, give—like Oprah handing out cars—but without bankrupting yourself. You'll trigger Dr. Robert Cialdini's "reciprocity," and suddenly, people feel obligated to like you (or at least not ghost you).

It's not about hammering them with constant pitches—nobody likes that. Instead, remember this: curiosity equals love, and love is basically the nuclear reactor of the universe. Most consultants and coaches fail because they're about as curious as a houseplant. Shift polarity. Get curious. Stop being boring. Simple, right?

I'm currently coaching a new coach who's transitioning from being a top AE (because obviously crushing quotas wasn't hard enough, so why not tackle *coaching*?). Here's a snippet from our actual conversation as he scales the first Great Wall of Coaching: "Nobody wants a coach… until they do."

He's already getting meetings, landed his first referral, and even got an inbound lead just by posting—so yeah, he's doing laps around most newbies. He's got three meetings set for next week, which, let's be honest, is ahead of the curve. But, of course, he's still freaking out that his outbound game isn't perfect yet. Have no fear; it will be. Rome wasn't built in a day, and neither was a six-figure coaching business… but hey, anxiety's just part of the charm, right?

80/20: Buyers Sweat, You Collect

JM: "You did 6K, then 12K. Take everything you learned in the last two weeks and repeat it. What were the 20% of your actions that yielded 80% of your results? Double and triple down on those."

Client: "Well, one was a referral, and one was inbound. I still need to get a cold outbound close, which scares me."

JM: "You need to overcome that for sure. Treat all the first meetings the same, whether referrals, inbounds, or outbound. Just run the *7-step Close Process*, trust it to convert, and create a polarity shift. I see inbound and outbound identically.

Imagine this: someone is 50 lbs overweight. They see an advertisement and contact the personal trainer who gets people fit. Results as calling cards! Whether they get contacted by the trainer who walks up to them at the gym (outbound) or see an ad (inbound), it doesn't matter. They are 50 lbs overweight. Pain is there, demand is there.

All you're doing is tapping into the *existing demand*. Applied to sales, this means they have a pipeline problem, a progression problem, or a closure problem.

According to the Chet Holmes pyramid, 3 in 100 are in the window. 40 in 100 will entertain switching or check you out, which is relatively high.

Client: All the people I have worked with have either talked to Johnny Mnemonic or bought his course previously.

Me: Oh, that's a good thing – *buyer's buy!* People who have previously bought sales training buy more. It's just like dating apps: collect them all. It's easier to close (aka enroll!) people who already understand/see value in this.

Master Coach Rich Litvin (trained by Steve Chandler) advocates creating a tracker to measure your prospecting progress. It's this simple, and it works. Read *The Prosperous Coach*.

What to track per Rich Litvin (create a dashboard):

1. Connections: How many people did you connect with this week?

2. Invitations: How many people did you invite to a coaching conversation?
3. Coaching Experiences: How many people did you coach - who are not current clients?
4. No's: How many no's did you collect?
5. Proposals: How much money did you request?"

Outflow equals inflow—it's like fishing, but with less patience and more PDFs. The more proposals you toss out into the world, the more invoices will come reeling back, flapping their little wings of revenue. Proposals lead to invoices, invoices lead to closes, and closes wink at you on their way back around, completing the virtuous cycle.

Think of it as *catch-and-release fishing*. No harpoons, no wrestling marlins, and definitely *no. hard. sell.*

Unlock the flywheel step by step—it's so simple it'll make your brain hurt. Simple doesn't mean easy, but hey, you've got this. Grab the net, cast wide, and watch the magic happen.

Challenge: Will you ask 1,000 people? If 100% of people say no, you need to ask more. "You can have anything in life you want if you're willing to ask 1,000 people." (Byron Katie)

Pro Tip: You can send your proposal as a sleek email with a few bullet points—short, snappy, and to the point. Or, if you're feeling fancy, whip up a shared Google Doc, slap on a "Goals and Metrics" section, and tag your prospect like you're playing tag in the business playground. Bonus: Let them edit it because nothing says "we're in this together," like collaborative document chaos.

After your first Zoom call, memorialize the conversation ASAP—like it's the last avocado toast at Mimosa brunch. If needed, hop on a second call to wrestle their objections to the ground in real-time. Are you feeling good about the deal? Skip the awkward silence and fire off an invoice through Bill.com or Stripe.

And remember: *Stop obsessing about closing.* Instead, channel your inner therapist. Dive deep, listen harder than a Spotify algorithm, and figure out how to help them. Jonny Staker, a high-ticket coach/client, summed it up best: "Detach from the sale." (Newsflash: That's how you win it.)

Troubleshooting Moment: One of my clients created a founder-led sales school priced at $5K annually. After 75 calls, he discovered every founder had the same budget: zero dollars. Why? He was targeting broke founders instead of funded ones. Once he started chasing post-seed or A-round founders, magic happened. Suddenly, my *JMM*™ techniques sliced through objections like Gordon Ramsay with a steak knife. He's now thriving as a Fractional CRO. Moral of the story: Your Ideal Client Profile (ICP) isn't just a fun acronym—it's your survival guide.

Also, stop aiming for Account Executives (AEs) just because you were a top AE and feel *seen*. Here's the cold, hard truth: 60-80% of AEs live paycheck-to-paycheck. Sure, they can scrape together $300/month or $3K/year, but they're not your dream client if you're selling premium coaching. Want their money? Go up the ladder—target their bosses or infiltrate Enablement to unlock Learning & Development budgets. Pro tip: These budgets typically range from $1.5-$5K/year/rep... until Salesforce decides to cancel them, as they just did. But I'm sure they'll be back. Thanks, Uncle Marc.

Final Wisdom: My old Salesforce boot camp trainer, Todd Caponi, dropped this gem in 2012: "The purpose of any step in a sales process is to get to the next step." If they ghost you, go dark, or stall like a middle school group project, drag them back to their "why" and onto another call.

And let's not forget Townsend Wardlaw's golden rule: A healthy coaching business thrives on 5-10 discovery calls per week. So, write it down. Stick it on your fridge. Tattoo it on your forearm if you have to.

CHAPTER 3

Starting Strong - Get Clients Early

"THE SEX & CASH THEORY - The creative person basically has two kinds of jobs: One is the sexy, creative kind. Second is the kind that pays the bills. Sometimes the task in hand covers both bases, but not often."

– Hugh MacLeod

People come to me daily, wanting to escape the 9-to-5 grind and launch their own coaching or consulting biz, but they're stumped on finding that first client. My philosophy? Clients are everywhere. Out of 2.3 billion adults on this planet, 11 million are in sales, and 400 million are small business owners. They are legion; you are...well, *one*. That feeling of scarcity? It's as real as Bigfoot.

A quick scroll through Amazon's endless pages on "coaching" or "side hustles" might feel like swimming with sharks. But here's the kicker: the opportunity ocean isn't bloody—it's blue. The clients are out there waiting for you to dive in, even if you need a steel cage.

The pie keeps growing; statistically, you've got more clients than you could ever handle. In 2024, the coaching industry was set to hit $6.2 billion, up from $2.8 billion in 2019. That's a 17% growth rate, people! The average coach charges $244 an hour, and the executive coaching market alone will be worth $27 billion by 2032. And that's just the beginning: a third of all Fortune 500 companies use executive coaches, and traditional consulting services are now valued at a trillion bucks a year.

Meanwhile, boomers are passing on $68 trillion to their kids, and by 2025, millennials will make up 75% of the global workforce. Translation: there are clients with cash to burn and dreams to build. Statistically, one out of every 100 prospects can quickly swing your premium fee. So there's no excuse—you can reach them if they're out there.

And remember: anything worth closing is worth chasing. *JMM Rule #467!*

Yes, we can passively wait for synchronicity to bring clients our way. But imagine this: spotting someone you admire, reaching out in the moment, sparking a meaningful conversation, uncovering a challenge or opportunity, and *actively* creating that client relationship.

Some of the best things in my life I hunted down, and some of the worst showed up randomly inbound as happenstance. Good things come to those who wait. I'm open to spending 10 years going after something I genuinely want: patience in the manifestation.

The eternal tug-of-war between *chasing* and *attracting* is one of those paradoxes you must live with—like loving tacos but hating the mess. Here's the kicker: the word *action* is hiding in *ATTRACTION*. Coincidence? Nope. Welcome inbound leads like gravy on Thanksgiving, but don't count on them to fill your plate. This book's outbound conversational techniques? That's your turkey.

Don't wait. Seriously, stop reading this and create a client right now. Like, right *now*. Reach out and converse with a quality human (not your cousin on Facebook trying to sell you essential oils). And for the love of all things holy, don't try to *sell coaching*. You're not hawking vacuum cleaners door-to-door... yet! Look for a problem you can solve or grab an opportunity, like a free Costco sample.

Ask yourself, "How can I serve?" Spoiler alert: Serving wins every time. And you don't even have to wear an apron.

First Circle Exercise

Make a list in a spreadsheet of the following:

1. How many connections are there in your cell phone? Who could you advise/consult/coach now?
2. How many 1st degrees are on LinkedIn?
3. Reach out to them with a lateral referral ask that sounds unassuming like this: "Hey Jane, I'm starting to do some coaching on the side; maybe that applies to you. Who do you know?"

The beauty of this strategy is that if it's relevant, people will *self-select* and pop into your inbox with, "Hey, could you help me?" Or, even better, they'll refer you to others faster than your mom tells her friends about your latest achievement.

And here's the thing—don't be stingy with your referral payouts. I used to offer a measly 10% discount coupon, but then I heard

Russell Brunson is out here giving 30% like he's Santa Claus. So, I bumped mine up to 20%, and guess what? Some absolute legend in Australia sent me $90,000 in referrals. $90K! Mate, that's enough to fund an endless supply of Tim Tams and kangaroo rides.

First Circle Referral Exercise

1. List every contact in your phone that could make a referral
2. List everyone on LinkedIn who could
3. Now, ask for referrals and offer 20%. "Hey Jim, I'm doing some advising and know you're well connected; if you know any sales leaders who need to double their pipeline and you make an intro, I'm happy to give you 20%."

Second Circle & Advanced Sales Navigator Tactics

100% of your new business comes from your views. That's right—your profile views are a goldmine, so mine every single one of them like you're digging for diamonds in Minecraft. Add and message all the relevant people. That's the jackpot.

Step 1: Watch your profile views like a hawk on too much coffee.

Step 2: Respond immediately, as your life depends on it.

Step 3: Be blunt, bold, and a little provocative in your outreach—not desperate. You're sparking curiosity, not begging for attention.

Mining your first —and second-degree connections is like having X-ray vision for networking. Look for nodes—like Scott Leese and me, who are connected to 30,000 people and probably know every thought leader, influencer, and cool kid in your space. Nodes are power hubs. Find them and use them.

Pro Tip: Mine *everyone* who likes, comments on your posts, views your profile, or follows you. I've gotten so much business from lurkers who never even engaged publicly. Views *are* business. Period.

Want to turbocharge? *Commenting beats posting.* Find a post where your prospects are hanging out, leave a comment *acknowledging and provoking*, and then reply to two other comments below yours. Do this 10 times a day, and voilà—you've created a snowball that'll eventually turn into an inbound avalanche.

Fun fact: Most people lurk like double agents—they love your book, webinar, or offer but won't engage. Why? Because your competitor isn't another coach or consultant—it's "do nothing" (shoutout to Tony J. Hughes). People default to the status quo. Your job? Nudge them out of it.

Want scale? Use Sales Navigator like a pro:

- LinkedIn 1st-degree messages: 50/day. Copy. Paste. Pray.
- InMails: 50/month.
- Open Profile InMails: 800/month (thank you, loopholes).
- Test your messaging on Open Profiles and use the green dot to see who's online (like digital stalking, but make it business-friendly).
- Use all your monthly InMails—it's not rollover data; if you don't use it, you lose it. I blow through mine by the 16th and frequently uncover $50,000 in hidden deals.

Pro-level LinkedIn hacks:

- Filter 2nd-degree connections through nodes like Josh Braun. With ~400 mutual connections, you look like a rockstar with clout.

- Sort searches by "posted on LinkedIn" and exclude "People you interacted with" to avoid repeat mistakes.
- Save this search, rinse, repeat.

Oh, and don't underestimate the blank connection request. Mystery is sexy. If your profile's new, though, maybe tailor it just a smidge.

Every missed profile view, unmined connection, and unused InMail is *leaving money on the table*. The opportunity cost is massive. The reward is bigger than your Bitcoin wallet after 2013.

Sales Navigator Spears (Outbound)

Key distinction: Use "sparks" for first-degree connections—short, engaging chat flows that assume familiarity and *spark* instant rapport. For second-degree connections, adopt a "spear" approach inspired by *JMM*™ cold emails, leveraging variable subject lines (see JMM 1.0 for reference). Experiment with ultra-short InMails, exploring a range of strategies—from bold, direct asks to softer, lateral, and indirect approaches across both channels.

Generally, the first degree works more like a soft sell chat.

When it comes to InMail (2nd degree), you've got one shot—so make it count. The key heuristics I rely on are quantified social proof, brevity, and emotional resonance rooted in pain or fear. A strong InMail starts with a compelling case study highlighting clear ROI with concrete proof points. (Check out real examples of high-impact InMail spears below!)

Heuristics are powerful shortcuts—formulas, and frameworks that form the foundation of the most effective templates. Think of them as the "meta" of strategic linguistics.

Example Heuristics*

1. brevity
2. specificity
3. social proof
4. differentiated value prop (IP)
5. fear/pain emotional resonance
6. story
7. soft CTA
8. tap out
9. bs alarm

*Read Sales Superpowers (JMM 1.0) and the Codices for a complete dissertation on JMM Copywriting.

Get the Codices and other book bonuses by going to: SalesSuperpowers.com/bonus

Example 2nd Degree Open Profile "Spears" (Sales Nav)

Subject: growth
Body: Hey Name – Helping sales leaders dramatically increase pipeline with counterintuitive techniques I developed; worth exploring?

Subject: first name (lower case)
Body: I help leaders 5X pipeline; worth exploring?

Subject: scrappy
Body: Hey Name, I just worked with a client who does Design-as-a-Service to unlock 15 net new meetings with unusual GIFs. Are you going outbound yourself to generate clients?

Here's a complex, direct spear with a Heuristics-based approach from *JMM 1.0*. It's concise, social proof-based, and specific. Note: It got a positive response!

Subject: 75K/mo
Body: Name—What if you could attract coaching clients with reverse psychology in DMs? My frameworks generated $336K solo in July, with clients hitting $75K months. After previewing JMM 4.0, a top trainer signed up for my full-fee coaching. This exclusive model is for coaches ready to 2-5X their business. worth exploring?

(The lowercase typo is on purpose; it makes it look more human!)

Note that over 50 connections in common is good for "optics" and builds immediate credibility.

"Those damn spears work!"– Donie

The one he used in InMail:

Subject: Running minus alcohol?
Body: Hey Richard, going sober has been one of my best decisions ever. There is no guarantee I can help, and you may not be interested. I help founders close more sales. Is it worth having a conversation to see if I can help?

Note: On the first try, my celebrity client set a CRO meeting with a short spear in Navigator, yielding a $25K deal.

Stealth Hustle–Success Under the Radar

If you're a coach or consultant struggling to gain traction, here's the unfiltered truth: get a side gig or even a full-on job. Why? Because when you're not sweating bullets to close every client like it's the last donut on earth, you suddenly exude this fabulous, calm confidence clients can practically smell. With a steady paycheck, the desperate "I need this sale" vibes evaporate. Instead, you're coaching from a place of zen, not caffeine-fueled survival mode.

Think of it like this:

1. Got a corporate job? Use that salary as a cushion, and let your side hustle breathe.
2. Side hustle sinking? Add a corporate gig to lower the stakes and make life (and clients) bearable.

During my last VP of Sales stint at a tech company, I nailed my work in the usual 5-7 hours a day and still had enough bandwidth to coach, advise, and throw in some motivational speeches (no, they didn't ask). I didn't slap "executive coach" or "sales wizard" on my LinkedIn, though; that's just begging for awkward questions from the boss. Keep it low-key: "GTM Advisor" does the trick nicely.

And yeah, the DMs can get a little weird. Sometimes, people flip the script: "Uh, Justin, why are you asking all these questions? How can I help *you*?" I just said I was a SaaS VP doing minor advising. Most companies won't bat an eye at "GTM Advisor" or "Subject Matter Expert" in your headline as long as you're not too obvious about moonlighting as the next Tony Robbins.

The key is to get creative with the job title—think "specialist," "process guru," "facilitator," "mentor," or "problem solver." It's all about striking that balance where you're undercover enough to keep HR happy but bold enough to make your DM game strong. Then, subtly align this mysterious yet impressive title with your messaging. Before you know it, you're living the double life with style.

Pro Tip: Let's talk about the word "coach." People claim to hate it—but let's be real; they also hate cold calls and still pick up the phone. Here's the deal: If you ask 1,000 people in a red ocean,

"Would you like some coaching, consulting, or training?" you'll get 1,000 "no thanks" responses faster than you can say, "Hard pass!" That's not coaching—that's clerking.

But here's why I still leave "executive coach" in my headline: it sets the frame. They see me as the coach and themselves as the client. This avoids role reversal, where suddenly *they're* coaching *you*—a disaster for authority. If that happens, flip it back like an Aikido master and keep the coaching frame intact. (Shoutout to Litvin and Chandler for that gem.)

Fun fact: You can fully engage someone without ever saying the word "coach." Focus on their goals, problems, opportunities, and what's holding them back. When I slide into the DMs with, "Would you like some help with that?" they *know* I'm offering coaching; there's no need to say it. But if I just call myself "Advisor"? That's when I get "What's up? How can I help you?" Stick with "coach"—you'll attract warmer, more ready-to-buy prospects.

Of course, test it. A/B your headlines to see which generates less role reversal and better lead quality.

Side Hustle Survival:

If you're building a coaching biz while working for a company, tread carefully. Some firms don't like reps dabbling in training, courses, or consulting and might slap your wrist (or worse). They think your intellectual property (IP) belongs to them, even if it's *your* genius on your *own* time. That's why you must consult a lawyer before getting too deep. Look for sketchy clauses like IP assignments or confidentiality agreements that claim ownership of your ideas.

Here's your goal: carve out the IP you create on your own time. Document timelines, keep it off company devices, and make sure you own your frameworks. It's your right to write a book, build a course, and establish your voice—don't let anyone steal that.

If all goes smoothly, you'll pick up a few clients for $2.5K/month. Remember, $5K/month is $60K/year, just from a side hustle. Add that to your full-time gig, and boom—you're printing money.

Russian Doll Hustle

The Matryoshka, or Russian nesting doll, metaphor explains precisely how to monetize your skills. One doll fits inside another: *Who is your client?* Start with *yourself*. If you were a rep, you would coach reps. If you led teams, you would coach team leaders or run workshops. Layer by layer, you would monetize your skills like the blades on a Gillette razor.

Here's my Theory of Everything:

1. Who is Sarah?
2. What are Sarah's skills?
3. What was Sarah's journey in building those skills?

Sarah finds more "Sarahs" and accelerates them on their path. That's the magic: your coaching is a microcosm of your skills, story, and accomplishments.

How to Monetize Your Role Today:

Think of your current job as a sales pipeline for your coaching business. Whatever you're doing now, that's what you coach.

- Leading a sales team? Coach clients on creating pipelines, closing deals, and strategizing more effectively.
- Full-cycle sales? Package enablement programs for AEs.
- Running a top-of-funnel team? Advise SDR leaders and target Heads of Demand Gen or Sales Enablement.

It's all about moving the right metrics:

- Create Pipeline
- Push deal flow to 3-5X the target ($10M pipeline at 20% close rate = $2M closed-won)
- Speed up deal velocity
- Increase ACV (Annual Contract Value) or TC (Total Contract Value)

That's your diamond—polish it and start cashing in.

CHAPTER 4

Time Mastery - Balance, Burnout-Proofing & Building Like a Boss

"When you do more than you're paid for, eventually you will get paid for more than you do."

— Zig Ziglar

Imagine feeling stuck and disconnected from your core—like your soul's Wi-Fi signal just hit a dead zone. This could mean one of your Ikigai areas is buffering. *Ikigai*, the Japanese concept meaning "reason for being," is the life coach you didn't know you needed.

Now, picture four circles: Passion, Mission, Profession, and Vocation. When they align, it's like finding the cheat code for a meaningful, fulfilled life. When they don't? Well, you're probably binge-watching *Breaking Bad*, wondering why nothing feels right.

Ikigai isn't some mystical mumbo-jumbo; it's practical alignment. Think of it as a life GPS powered by a four-circle Venn diagram that answers essential questions like, "Why do I get up in the morning?" and "Can I enjoy my job without hating Mondays?"

1. **What You Love** – The things that spark joy and excitement.
2. **What the World Needs** – Your contribution to society and positive impact.
3. **What You Can Be Paid For** – How you earn a living.
4. **What You Are Good At** – Your skills and unique talents.

Where two circles intersect, a deeper layer of insight emerges:

- **Passion** = What You Love + What You Are Good At
- **Mission** = What You Love + What the World Needs
- **Profession** = What You Are Good At + What You Can Be Paid For
- **Vocation** = What the World Needs + What You Can Be Paid For

At the center of these circles lies your *Ikigai*—the culmination of all four dimensions. This is your *being* in its purest form. It's why you leap out of bed each morning and stay committed until you've seen your work through.

Alignment requires ongoing refinement, especially as you progress through life's stages. Neglecting one or more areas creates an imbalance. You may end the day feeling busy yet unfulfilled, sensing that you are missing something vital. Miss two or more, and you may feel a nagging anxiety, an inner reminder that you're not fully aligned with your purpose.

Take time to fill in these circles with specifics. For example:

- **What You Love** – Perhaps you love guiding people to become better leaders and using music to enhance their well-being.

- **What You Are Good At** – Your strengths could be leadership coaching and music production.
- **What the World Needs** – Mentally resilient, emotionally intelligent leaders are essential.
- **What You Can Be Paid For** – Executive coaching programs integrating music for stress reduction and mental clarity.

When these circles intersect, you discover new layers:

- **Passion** – You merge your love for leadership with your music talent, creating an experience that enhances clarity and well-being.
- **Mission** – Your goal is to develop emotionally grounded leaders through music-based coaching.
- **Vocation** – Providing leadership coaching supported by music therapy to help leaders thrive emotionally.
- **Profession** – Offering paid programs where leadership meets music for mental clarity and stress relief.

This is how Ikigai defines *you*. You're not just a coach or a music producer; you're a unique blend—a guide for leaders who tap into the power of music to create balance and resilience. This alignment doesn't just clarify your purpose; it becomes a practical filter for your work, highlighting where adjustments might be needed to stay true to your core *being*.

The Japanese are a trip—in the best way possible. They've got this thing called *Kintsugi*, which is basically the art of taking broken stuff and gluing it back together with gold or silver. Imagine dropping your favorite bowl, and instead of crying about it, you fix it up so it's a Kardashian-level glow-up. Now, it's not just a bowl—it's a bowl *with a story*. IKEA could never.

So, be like a phoenix rising from the ashes—or better yet, like that phone screen you shattered but turned into a cool conversation starter. Let this book be your golden glue. Because sometimes the road to your dreams feels less like a scenic highway and more like wading through a swamp in Crocs. But hey, progress is progress.

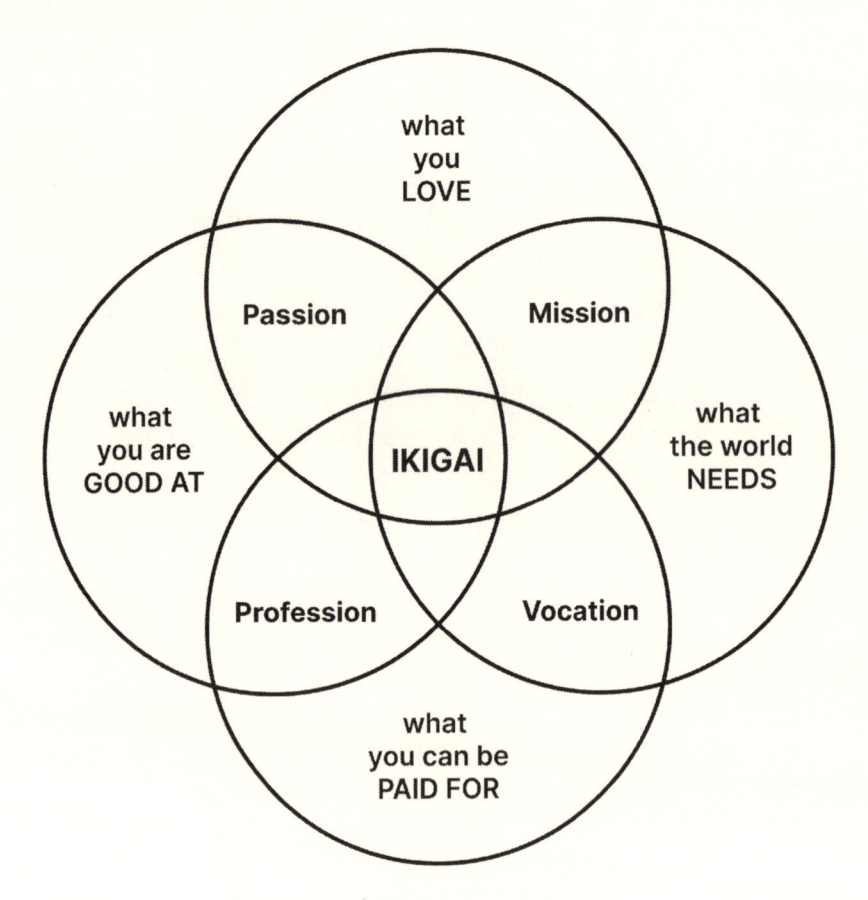

Dennis Bodor and Emmy van Deurzen

As Ernest Hemingway wisely said, "The world breaks everyone, and afterward, many are strong at the broken places." Or, as Kahlil Gibran might have put it, "Your scars are just receipts for character development." Translation? You're overdue for a plot twist, and it's going to be epic.

Profit with Purpose: Earn More, Live Balanced

With the strategies in this book, you'll be ready to rake in $250-500K a year, working just 25 hours a week as a full-time coach or consultant. Once you hit seven or multiple seven figures, you might see those hours climb back to 50+. Remember those 70-hour weeks just to scrape by on $45K? Is there anyone you can think of who *hasn't* sold shoes, waited tables, or clocked in at some hourly gig? We've all been there. Most of us didn't roll out of bed to a six-figure salary with a bow. So if you can land it, "Nice work if you can get it."

People often ask, "Justin, why wouldn't you create courses and assets to MMWYS—make money while you sleep?" I don't mind clocking five hours daily and making $100-300K monthly. Besides, I'd probably wake up in a panic thinking, "Is the money making itself, or is it just hiding under the mattress?"

Tips for High Hourly Earnings and Work-Life Balance (With Extra Zest)

1. **Never Work by the Hour—It's Unethical (and Kinda Dumb).**

   Alan Weiss said it best: if you pay me by the hour, I'm incentivized to stretch out the clock like a soap opera finale. Want me at $2,000/hr while I take 50 hours to solve a 5-hour problem? Sure, it sounds great—for me. Instead, let's focus on ROI and results. Case in point: if I'm paid $5,000 monthly for eight 30-minute sessions (4 hours total), that's $1,250/hr on paper. I'll even "burn" it down to $500/hr to over-deliver. I might toss in a surprise 1:1 just for kicks. But the key here is always protecting your hourly calculus like it's the last slice of deep-dish pizza.

2. **Block Nights and Weekends.**

   Going full cowboy, coaching 24/7, sounds cool—until it doesn't, and you're crying into your third coffee at 2 a.m., Googling "signs of burnout." Take weekends off to hang with your family, rank nationally at Pickleball, or just stare at your crypto balance. Bonus points if you're resting, reading Nietzsche, and plotting world domination on your days off.

3. **Exercise = Sanity.**

   The holy trinity: 10,000 steps, lifting heavy things, and not eating like a wise guy after a prison break. Exercise saves you from becoming that jittery, over-caffeinated coach who "just loves the grind." Pun intended! Speaking of caffeine...

4. **Limit the Liquid Lightning.**

   Caffeine is great for alertness—until you're ten Red Bull shots deep and vibrating like a cartoon character. Stay creative by slowing down and letting your brain chill in alpha and theta states that tap your deep creative subconscious, where magic (and ESP-level client insights) happen. And if you're extra fancy, toss on some Solfeggio tones like 432 or 528 Hz to align your chakras. Science says it's legit; if nothing else, it sounds cool.

5. **Get Outside (Yes, Really).**

   Go barefoot on a beach, dunk in a lake, or hug a tree. "Earthing" is the new pink! Reset your DNA with some Schumann resonance vibes (look it up—it's a thing).

Sure, it sounds woo-woo, but spend a day in nature, and suddenly, you're having life-changing insights like, "I should absolutely pitch this new offer!" Nature: 1, Hustle Culture: 0.

6. **Obsess Over Clients (In a Healthy Way).**

Here's the secret: close fewer clients, but treat them like you're their personal DJ. What tracks (or insights) can you drop to get them hyped? How can you remix their strategy to blow their minds? If you've got 10-25 clients, keep a playlist and spin new ways to crank up their results daily. Be their DJ Khaled—always another one.

And stop hogging the mic. Coaches who shut up and listen—like therapists who don't charge by the hour—will obliterate the mansplainers. Watch Rich Litvin's 100 videos and take notes like it's your final exam.

Work smart, stay human, and remember: sometimes the best breakthroughs happen when you're barefoot in the woods or deep into your 5th cat video of the day. Productivity? Overrated. Cat memes? Timeless.

Speaking of random segues, let's talk about the magic of green— my favorite color (totally not biased by my eyes or my wallet). Ever notice how hanging around trees, grass, or even that sad houseplant clinging to life instantly chills you out? That's because green is basically nature's Prozac. Science says it lowers stress, cranks up the zen, and works faster than doom-scrolling Twitter during a meltdown.

Our ancestors hardwired us to love green because it screamed, "Hey, food! Water! No hungry tigers!" Even *looking* at plants tricks your brain into thinking, "We're safe. Chill out." That's why hospitals paint walls green—it's not for the decor vibes, it's for the *don't freak out* vibes.

And green doesn't just calm you; it makes you sharper. Ever hit a mental brick wall, then take a walk and suddenly channel Einstein? That's green spaces decluttering your brain, like Marie Kondo, but for your thoughts. It's a reset button for your mind—Ctrl+Alt+Delete, but make it leafy.

You don't need a rainforest to feel the magic. A desk plant, a window view, or even a budget-friendly nature screensaver can turn your workspace from a "stress pit" to a "zen oasis." So, get a plant (yes, fake counts), hug a tree, or give your lawn some loving eye contact. Green: the life hack your soul's been waiting for.

Business Foundations—LLCs, Corps, and Smart Finances

Quick disclaimer: I'm not a CPA or attorney, so consult a qualified pro for all the CYA stuff.

When I got my first check from a Mark Wahlberg venture, I realized I needed to level up from "Hey, write the check to Justin Michael" to something legit. Enter *Justin Michael Consulting*—if you name your business after yourself, you skip the "doing business as" (DBA) drama. Top trainers like Scott Leese do this, too. Sometimes, your name is your best brand (and it fits perfectly on a check).

As my business grew, I upgraded from H&R Block to a CPA and a genius M&A attorney. Now I'm running a California S Corp with tax write-offs galore—home office, mileage, subcontractors, you name it. Fun fact: small businesses make up 99% of all companies, so being one comes with perks. Just don't forget to document *everything*. Use tools like Bill.com and QuickBooks, get an employer identification number (EIN) from Uncle Sam, and link it to payment platforms like Stripe, Payoneer, Wise, or Zelle.

Pro Tip: The more ways you can collect money, the better.

Consider setting up a limited liability corporation (LLC) or a Nevada/Delaware C Corp. That would be a great move. You can even go international—England has a Ltd., and Australia has a Pty. Need a tax wizard? Hit me up; I know a guy.

E&O insurance (Errors and Omissions): get it. It's your business-world safety net, covering your back when a client claims you missed something and decides to lawyer up. Even shaky claims can cost you big. Without it, one lawsuit could drain your bank account and make your spouse seriously regret marrying you.

Now, about scaling: sure, you can hire contractors, SEO freelancers, editors, and even sub-trainers. But if you're chasing premium clients? *Do it all yourself.* I don't automate or delegate my coaching. It's always me because my craft is bespoke—like a LaFerrari supercar. When you pay $1,250-$2,000/hour, you get 24 years of expertise tailored to you.

One of my favorite lines? "We switch lives. I take your chair, and together we crack your funnel." That's priceless. So, document everything, insure your business, and remember: artisan coaching is like the thousand-year-old craft of Samurai swordsmithing. And no, I don't outsource *artisanal*.

SECTION II

Prospecting & Conversion–Client Acquisition Magic

CHAPTER 5

Breaking Barriers To Overcome Client Hurdles

"We must create the desire in the prospect."

– Garrett "GMAC" MacDonald

Exactly. You take the leap—quit the 9-to-5, carve out your niche, craft the perfect offer, speed read *$100M Offers*, and...crickets. "Curse you, Alex Hormozi!" you shout into the universe. But no one's biting on your coaching offer. Why? Because the coaching industry is packed to the brim—10,000 trainers, gurus, experts, and folks with too many LinkedIn posts clawing for attention. Welcome to the ultimate red ocean.

But here's the kicker: there *is* a way to stand out from the noise. Enter *The 4th Frame*. Everyone keeps asking me for the advanced version and better openers. Well, buckle up—because I'm finally spilling the goods right here.

Fourth Frame (Advanced Training)

History lesson:

1. Sell a product
2. Sell time
3. Sell ROUTE (Matrixed)
4. Converse (sell by chat!)

Technique: You stay focused on

1. The problem/opportunity
2. Curious about their world / their profile
3. Injecting yourself into the solution toward that future state

And just fixate on 1 and 2 back-to-back until they crack and the polarity *shifts*. There's no rocket science here. It's an elemental detective, doctor, and therapist archetype and entirely removes showing off.

The Polarity Shift is the holy grail of selling. It's the precise moment when your idea moves to their idea—that subtle moment when desire jumps the shark (or the couch, Tom Cruise!)

But does the *4th frame* work? Let's ask Luke Shalom:

> "Since we worked together, I used JMM to scale my business from $2K p/m to $25K p/m in 5 months. I closed $172k in my first year in business, blowing my expectations out of the water. The numbers don't lie. I would have paid 10X the investment for how much of an impact working with JM had on my life, confidence, and business."

The 3 Walls

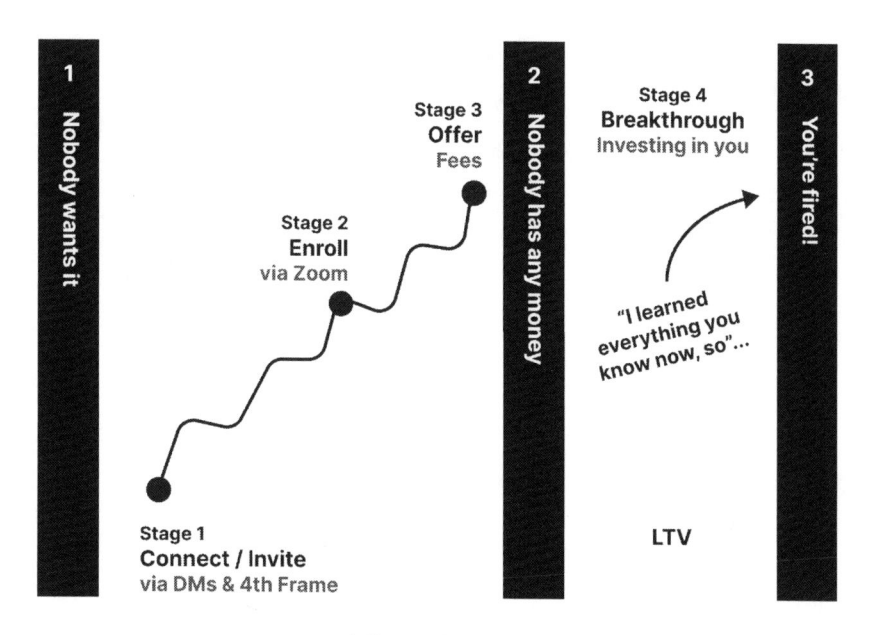

```
1: Nobody wants it
2: Nobody has any money
3: You're fired!

Stage 1: Connect / Invite — via DMs & 4th Frame
Stage 2: Enroll — via Zoom
Stage 3: Offer — Fees
Stage 4: Breakthrough — Investing in you
"I learned everything you know now, so"...
LTV
```

Phil Smith Design

Wall One: Nobody wants coaching.

Wall Two. Nobody has any money.

"I'll have to think about it"—the kiss of death. It hits you like a freight train right after you've just listened to your prospect spill their soul in DMs and had your first call with the patience of a monk. You sit there, pretending to be calm and heart-centered, while your world crumbles into a thousand tiny shards, like a baby elephant on a rampage in a Ming vase shop.

But here's the thing: we don't crumble under pressure—we coach every client *through* their breakthrough. That cave they're terrified to enter? The one where they finally invest in you? Yep, that's where the treasure's stashed: massive success (and probably a few emotional cobwebs). Think of it like clearing a forest for new growth—we've got to air out their trauma from past dud coaching experiences, like opening the windows after your partner turns "date night mahi-mahi" into a smoke signal.

Then, we hit them with the *7-step Close Process*. Suddenly, they're chasing your fee like they just put it all on red at the roulette table—hearts pounding, chips flying, and praying for a jackpot.

> *"People love to buy, but they hate to be sold."*
> *– Jeffrey Gitomer*

Per Rich Litvin: "We invest in coaching for three reasons:

1. **To increase our income**
2. **To increase our influence**
3. **To increase our impact.**"

7 Steps O

1. Goal
2. The goal behind the goal
3. What else have you tried?
4. What's holding you back?
5. Case study
6. Polarity shift (What does it cost?)
7. Share fees tied to ROI of #1

Grab a Post-it, scribble this down, and slap it on your mirror or laptop—your shrine, your rules. It's not science; it's sorcery. After a thousand tries, I figured it out, and the same magic formula kept showing up. Let's look at it from a different lens:

1. Where are you going? (Hopefully, somewhere better than "away from here.")
2. Pressure test their goal—because, shocker, it's *never* about the money.
3. Banish their bad coach baggage. (No holy water required.)
4. Get them to admit their kryptonite—preferably without tears.
5. Share your highlight reel—and your clients' Oscar-worthy transformations.
6. Play it right, and this part's on autopilot. Caution: Curiosity killed the cat—don't bite on earlier fee questions.
7. End with possibility, never affordability (Chandler/Litvin), not "Do I need to sell my soul or audition for *Magic Mike*?"

Here's the thing: always tie your fees to their dream ROI. People will happily blow $10K on crypto if they think it'll turn into $100K overnight. Real high-performance coaches? We own the ROI talk but don't make promises—because we're coaches, not fortune tellers. My line? "I guarantee my time and expertise. If you bring the hustle, I'll bring the muscle."

Here's your golden ticket: *customization*. It's the coaching world's "open sesame" for high fees. Drop it into the conversation enough, and suddenly, you're not selling coaching—you're curating a bespoke, VIP-level transformation wrapped in velvet and delivered with a side of caviar.

Wall Three. Once they learn everything you know, you're fired.

My mentor, Bryan Franklin, who coached Reid Hoffman and somehow keeps clients for 2-5 years (yes, *years*), managed to hit $10MM in just three. One day, he drops this gem on me: "The more enigmatic, the higher the fee." That single line? It's made me millions. We'll dive into the magic behind it in this guide.

So, how do you keep clients returning and bump up that lifetime value (LTV) curve? Here's the catch: if you lay out every detail of your program in a statement of work (SOW), you're practically handing a playbook to the competition. Someone younger, hungrier, or with cheaper rent will swoop in and say, "I'll do exactly what Justin Michael does for half the price!" So, keep a little mystery in the mix—it's like sprinkling cayenne in a recipe. A hint of intrigue keeps them coming back for more.

Mystery keeps people hooked.

Scarcity makes them want it.

Exclusivity screams, "This is VIP, baby!"

And neediness? Well, that's just the romantic equivalent of texting "u up?" at 3 a.m. — don't do it.

Mark Manson said it best: "You will close clients directly in proportion to your level of *non-neediness*." Translation? Play it cool, not clingy.

Here's the kicker: once people crack your system, they'll be tempted to ghost you. "Awesome, I've mastered *The Justin Michael Method*. Byeee!" Unless...you keep evolving your game. Shake things up. Think of your coaching like an ad campaign— "Got milk?" was genius until it was *everywhere*. Don't let your methods go stale; keep them as fresh as your best ideas.

Always have new coaching plans locked and loaded for major milestones: funding rounds, CRO hires, product launches, or opening an office in a new region. Be ready to stick around through the twists and turns—like a trusted guide, not a one-hit wonder. Six months to two years is your sweet spot.

And here's the kicker: the better you get, the less you'll have to chase. Do your thing well, and warm referrals will parade in like you just took *Best in Show* at the Coaching Westminster.

The First Touch—DM Openers That Work

If I had to distill my entire client acquisition method—captured across seven books, six of which bear my name—it would come down to one game-changing principle:

The INDIRECT METHOD of client creation.

Prospects are fed up with the full-frontal sales approach. It's like hearing the same lousy pickup line on repeat. There are a hundred ways to spark engagement, and the possibilities become endless if you think laterally or indirectly. Start an organic conversation fueled by genuine curiosity. Then, ease into the *4th Frame*, the *7-Step*, or even layer them together. This isn't just sales—it's a sophisticated "strictly ballroom" dance that turns interest into action without ever making the first move.

Here's some incredible wisdom from Jonny Staker, one of my top clients who gets savage response rates, "There's no template for what works. The ultimate heuristic is being your genuine, authentic self. That's why it's about formulas and frameworks, *not* exact 'spark' openers. A/B test them and find out what lands and *why*. Riff around on limitless variations until you crack the top funnel on LinkedIn, and 80% respond."

For example, in music, artists must develop their style or "sound." Otherwise, you're derivative. Lenny Kravitz was critically panned and dismissed until he found his voice on his 5th album, "5." Don't be a clone using hacks and blind-click funnels. Acquire clients from the heart, the gut, and your intuition.

> *"Almost all potential coaching clients will show up in their first conversations with you as their biographical self only. Their ego. And that is the very habit that has kept them stuck and challenged. If you can help them with that and release them from that unnecessary straitjacket, you will be worth all the coaching money they can pay you."*
>
> *– Steve Chandler*

Openers That Pop:

- **PDF + Opinion Heuristic:** "Everyone has an opinion—how would you improve this content?" (Because people *love* to critique, and let's be real, it's easier than creating something original.)
- **Thread Sparker:** Ask a provocative question, "Is your sales team ready for 2025, or are we still playing 2020 ball?" (Page 177 of *Sales Superpowers*, SSP JMM 1.0—required reading, folks.)
- **Recruiter Mode:** Slide in with, "I noticed your move to [new role]. What motivated the jump?" Instant intrigue without the weird LinkedIn job spam vibes.
- **Activity Feed Goldmine:** "I saw your post about Q3 challenges—how are you planning to crush Q4?" (Specific and relevant = FIRE)

- **Transposing:** "Your [specific experience] reminds me of [my own experience]. Ever face [challenge]?" Relatability level: Expert.

Examples for the Brave:

- "Don't you think ChatGPT emails are just rep spam with a fancy hat?"
- "How's the Ray Dalio book working out? Worth my time?"
- "What inspired the Portugal gap year? Jealous over here!"

What NOT to Do:

- **Friend-Zoning Yourself:** If your headline doesn't scream "coach," you're just a "LinkedIn pen pal." Drop, "Have you ever worked with an executive coach?" and hold the frame—because Challengers take the trophy while Relationship Builders hold the door.
- **Flattery Bombs:** "Wow, congrats on the promotion and the award! Truly groundbreaking stuff..." said literally everyone else in your inbox.
- **Overuse First Names:** Don't be the guy who starts every sentence with 'Steve.' Unless, of course, you're auditioning to play a chatbot in a low-budget sci-fi. The biggest cringe? The name bump. Steve??
- **Pitch Slapping:** Nobody wants a cold DM that feels like a drunk pickup line at last call—spark a conversation that actually makes them want to say *yes*.

Notes & Hacks:

- **Metering:** Regulate your chatter. Don't hit back with a novel if their reply is ten words. Keep it punchy and show you listen.

- **Soft & Indirect Touches:** "Let's compare notes on the quarter." "Catch me up on your strategies." Trojan-horse into the conversation and save the heavy artillery (*7-Step Close*) for the call.

- **Troubleshooting:** Wide-open, human-level questions win: "How's the vibe at your company?" "Do you even *like* your boss?" You are guaranteed to get at least a smirk.

Autofill Hack:

- Hit the "Catch Up" tab and let LinkedIn AI sprinkle its generic magic: "Congrats on the new role!" or "Happy belated birthday!" Fire off 50 of these daily—it's not personalized, but people eat up recency bias like candy. Once they reply, pivot into 4th framing and hit them with the good stuff.

Out-of-the-Box Genius:

Picture this: a driving event at Porsche Experience Atlanta. Add AI magic to make your prospects into Will Ferrell as Ricky Bobby in *Talladega Nights*, sending custom video invites. It's fun, wild, and impossible to ignore - especially when CIOs suddenly have a full head of hair again. (Hat tip to JP Albano for showing us how to blend *JMM* with Stu Heinecke-style Contact Marketing like a pro.)

If your openers don't feel like a mic drop, go back and tweak 'em until they do.

CHAPTER 6

Sell By Chat - DM Your Way to Booked Calls

"Remember, you don't have to take yourself so seriously to do a seriously good job."

– Michael Neill

Imagine this: I get paid up to $2,000 an hour to teach people how to handle high-stakes DMs—where one wrong emoji could wreck a $25,000 deal faster than you can say, "Oops." Yep, that's right—a single rogue laughing emoji and your deal is toast. It's like flirting with a supermodel; it takes timing, charm, and the precision of a brain surgeon who's also having a really good hair day. Harsh but true.

Clients always ask, "What do I say? When? How often should I follow up before it's legally considered stalking?" Here's the deal—just like dating, if you hover too long, you'll start to smell like desperation. This is about the art of attraction, people! Bob, weave, throw in a dash of mystery. Do you drop the truth bomb or cushion it with empathy? My advice: channel your inner

Muhammad Ali. "Float like a butterfly, sting like a bee." And maybe throw in a bit of "Ghost them like Houdini."

Want to get good at this? Start with 500 honest conversations. Yep, there's no typo here. Dive in, swim through the awkward silences and cringe-worthy typos, and eventually, you'll develop a sixth sense. It's a superpower that whispers, "Now is the time to ask for the Zoom."

Let me blow up a myth: You don't need a Ph.D. in brand-building or a movie trailer of reels to get a client. All you need is one finger and a DM button. This is the *Justin Michael Method*: Stop hiding behind the inbound marketing Rose Parade float. Opportunity isn't politely waiting in line. It's banging on your DMs, yelling, "Why aren't you talking to me yet?!"

I know—you're itching to outsource this to some agency with a "guaranteed" lead-gen strategy. But here's the twist: people aren't buying a pitch; they're buying *you*. I don't care if you're a coach, a consultant, or an alpaca whisperer. Every elite coach I know still dives into their DMs, not just booking calls but crafting connections. They'll toss in an insight, a sprinkle of vulnerability, and leave the other person thinking, "Okay, I don't know if this is love, but I have to talk to you."

As Maya Angelou put it, people forget what you say but never forget how you make them feel. And that feeling is why they'll book the call and say, "Take my money."

Here's where it gets all Matrix-level philosophical. When you're fully present, the screen disappears. It's not just a DM exchange anymore; it's two humans having a real, honest conversation. No BS, just genuine curiosity. This is beyond selling; it's connecting.

Want to up your game? Read *The Game* by Neil Strauss and *Models* by Mark Manson. Yes, they're dating books, and the overlap is wild. It's true in dating and sales: neediness repels. If you're coming off like you need this call to make rent, they'll sense it and backflip out of there. Instead of a polished, Oscar-worthy DM, just send a raw message.

What is the biggest thing I've learned on this journey? Words are just the tip of the iceberg. Beneath every DM, there's an energy—an intent that people feel, like a vibe. The real magic happens when you're there just to connect and give value without strings attached. When you show up with calm confidence instead of "Oh please, let's chat," they lean in. They feel the difference and are drawn to you—not for what you're saying but for *why* you're saying it.

So, next time you're typing up a DM, ask yourself: What's my real intent here? You've just unlocked the cheat code when you make it about *connecting*, not closing.

You'll land more clients by being unapologetically real—sarcastic, funny, a little polarizing, and playing just hard enough to get—than by coming off like the overly eager puppy of the coaching world. No one hires the clingy "please like me!" energy; they hire the confident "you'll be lucky to work with me" vibe.

Be fearless. Speak the truth, but keep it classy, San Diego. Sometimes, that means having a blunt-but-loving "come-to-Jesus" chat:

- "Look, maybe wine isn't its own food group if you're serious about fitness."
- "You hate prospecting, never do it, and wonder why sales are slow. See the problem?"

The goal isn't to roast them; it's to show you care enough to tell them what they *need* to hear, not just what they *want* to hear.

Nobody invests in superficial, fake, happy-mask people-pleasing. Yet, many coaches are stuck in the "I'm nice, I'm helpful!" trap. Sure, you'll be beloved, praised... and broke, polishing up your corporate résumé. Or, you could take risks, speak the truth, change lives, and close high-fee clients who *actually respect you*.

Here's the deal: You need to live on the edge of "I'm scared of how they'll react" because that's where the magic happens. Think of it like this: are you the bartender or the personal trainer? The bartender pours your drinks till 3 a.m.; you forget their name by morning. The trainer charges $100 an hour, drags you out of bed at 5 a.m., yells at you sadistically to do another rep, and somehow, you *love* them for it. Be the trainer.

Drop the surface-level nice act. No one needs another LinkedIn love fest or "hope you're well!" DM. Act like you're already the coach with 35 clients paying $500 a session. Would that person have time to cold call or write sonnets in LinkedIn comments? Nope. Act *as if* you're already that person.

Here's the inconvenient truth: being "agreeable" won't make them trust you. If you don't call them out, push them out of their comfort zone, and challenge their lies (to you *and* themselves), they'll never see you as the person who can break them out of their rut. Every move you make to get them to "like you" just builds a second wall—the *money* wall. Instead, meet their excuses head-on.

When they start with, "I'm just not that kind of person" or "That could never work for me," call it out. "Is that true, or is that just your fear talking?" Look them in the eye (over Zoom) and hold up the mirror. You might be the *first* person who's ever done that for them.

I once had a client with a book, a retreat, and a solid method, yet he charged embarrassingly low fees. On the first call, I said, "*Nothing* about you, your business, or your method should hold you back from commanding top-tier fees. The only thing stopping you is your perception of your value." Five minutes in, *breakthrough*. He still calls that moment life-changing. Me? I was just speaking my mind.

Radical honesty gets results. Give people the breakthroughs they *need*, not the sugarcoated nonsense they *want*. Do this, and you'll never run out of clients who'll pay whatever you ask. They don't need a friend—they need a coach who can change their life.

"How do you handle the load?" clients ask. Simple: I don't work with toxic energy vampires. If talking to my clients doesn't feel like sipping espresso for my soul, they don't make the cut. I'm here to be energized, not exorcised.

Client Q: Is bumping, GIFing, and chasing low status lame? How do you avoid it?

A: If you do it with an IDGAF vibe—think *The Outsiders* cool, James Dean hair grease, or a Young Elvis pelvic twirl—you're golden. It's all about the *tone*. Writing, gifs, even punctuation—it all oozes intent. Care too much, and you're needy. Go out of your way, and you're desperate. But strut in like you just dropped a killer guitar solo and flipped the principal the bird, and now you're Billy Idol with a rebel yell? That's the secret sauce.

I get away with murder in my messaging because I love to provoke, and I'm genuinely detached from rejection. After 10,000 hours of cold calling and sending more emails than Gmail's server admins, rejection is just white noise.

And let's be honest—this stuff is Social Dynamics 101. It's dating but with money on the line. Robert Cialdini probably *did* wink at *The Game* during his psychology lectures. Frames, neuro-linguistic programming (NLP), micro-scripting—it's all Jedi mind tricks. Like dating, one misstep—a bad joke, a misread reply—and you're dead in the water. I've AB-tested enough chat flows to write the Napoleon Hill sequel *Chat and Grow Rich*.

Quick throwback: When I was 21, I worked in a call center. My job? Sell credit card insurance to people who lied about owning credit cards. Every American averages 3.84 cards, but ask them directly, and they'd say "No." The trick? Follow up with, "Which card do you *normally* use?" Nine out of ten would blurt, "Visa." I'd reply, "Great! It starts with a 4." Boom—converted. That's where I learned the power of tone and specificity. Jedi-level mind tricks that apply to any sales conversation.

Now, about client acquisition:

Newbies always ask, "Why not just pitch directly?" Because that's lazy order-taking, not client acquisition. Sure, you might luck out with in-market buyers, but swing buyers—the ambivalent majority—will ghost you faster than a bad Tinder date.

The swing buyers are where the gold is. Like swing voters in the Electoral College, they need to warm up. No pitch slaps like, "Why aren't you buying my course?" Instead, find out where they're stuck. What's their secret dream? What's holding them back? Be the first glimmer of hope they've seen in months. Pull them to Zoom, uncover their struggles, and flip the polarity.

Without this, you're stuck pitching thousands, praying 3% say yes. Sure, inbound works if you run $25K/month in ads and have a YouTube empire, but unless you're Russell Brunson, good luck. The middle majority is where the real game happens for the rest of us mortals. Convert the "meh" to "maybe," and you'll unlock a whole new tier of success.

Provoke. Flip the script. Be Lady Gaga, not the rando at karaoke night butchering "Bohemian Rhapsody."

Why *The 4th Frame*™ Works:

Let's face it—your prospects' brains are numb from all the identical LinkedIn pitches that start with "Hi [First Name], hope you're doing well!" That's why I created *The 4th Frame*™, a "chat and grow rich" technique that throws those clichés out the window. No names, no pleasantries—just a bold, subconscious jolt that grabs attention faster than a toddler with a drum set.

Proof? I've used this method to pull thousands of prospects to Zoom and close millions in 1:1 coaching and team workshops at $500-$2,000/hr. And every time I share this, people say, "Okay, but how exactly does it work?" Don't worry—actual excerpts of my threads are below. Spoiler: I don't ask, "How's your day?"

Blank Connects = Mystery:

Don't try to win them over with small talk. Just blank-connect and make sure your LinkedIn profile reads like a killer landing page: headline, About section, Featured—all WIIFM (*what's in it for them?*). Let your testimonials and big-name clients do the heavy lifting. If they check you out, they'll add you back. Then hit them with a THREAD SPARKER like:

"what's Q3 looking like for you?" (all lowercase, like you're too cool to care).

Skip the thank-you notes and polite intros. Provoke curiosity, shift gears, and pull to Zoom.

Tailoring Without Overthinking:

Should you tailor DMs? Sure—but don't overcomplicate it. Keep it simple:

- "How's Q3 shaping up compared to Q2?" works for anyone.
- "How are you optimizing your tech stack?" targets managers.

Throw in recent activity: "Big fan of Ray Dalio, too—thoughts on his latest podcast?" (Okay, maybe don't mention the Civil War prediction unless you're coaching doomsday preppers.)

Troubleshooting Too Many Freebies:

If you're drowning in first meetings with freebie seekers, qualify in the DMs. Tie your fees to ROI early:

When they ask, "What are your rates?" respond, "If someone's quoting fees in a DM, they're not the person you want. Let's hop on a call to figure out your needs. I've got packages for every budget."

Equity is Not Lunch Money:

Equity sounds sexy—until you're eating ramen and explaining to your kids why Monopoly money doesn't work at the grocery store. Only take equity if you're passionate about the mission *and* getting paid upfront. When someone says, "Can I pay you a percentage of the deals I close?" hit them with this:

"No. You're paying for my time, like hiring a competent attorney. Skin in the game = accountability to change. It *should* sting a little."

Spec Work? Red Flag City:

When asked to work on commission, I calmly reply: "If a coach agrees to work on pure commission, run. That's a red flag. Top coaches don't do that. I don't guarantee results—but I guarantee 24 years of experience and my full focus to crack your case. If you're serious, let's roll."

Bottom line? The *4th Frame* isn't just a strategy—it's your antidote to bland outreach. Provoke, connect, and watch your pipeline light up like a Vegas marquee.

DM Mastery—Formulas to Secure Meetings

Here's a game-changing framework to elevate your client acquisition: two systems, layered for maximum impact.

The 4th Frame
The 7-Step

They create a seamless approach that guides prospects from first interest to commitment. Use *the 4th Frame* to steer chat flows subtly and secure meetings, while *the 7-Step* drives each "first call" conversation with precision—uncovering goals, pain points, and the "why" that moves them. This unbeatable blueprint adapts in real-time, allowing you to toggle between direct and indirect approaches based on what resonates.

4th Frame:

1. Something personal on their LinkedIn profile
2. Something professional on their profile
3. Challenge/Opportunity
4. Something a machine wouldn't see on a profile (or via quick research)
5. Insert yourself into helping them. "Would you like some help with that?" – Rich Litvin

Or, "Is this something that you'd like to do?" - Steve Chandler

Formula: 1, 2, 1, 2, 3

Transposed over

Partial 7-step close process (if used in a DM):

1. Goal
2. The goal behind the goal / *"Money's never the goal; what's driving the money?" / your why?*
3. What else have you tried?
4. What's holding you back?
   – *Go for the Zoom meeting (drop your Calendly)*

Note: The precise moment you suggest a meeting and drop your calendar is "the flip" or "gear shift." It's a combination of gut instinct to know when to drop it. Typically, people chat too long.

Get some back and forth, like 3-5 DM pings and pongs, then flip early. Leave them wanting more.

YOU CAN USE 4TH FRAME OR 7 STEPS. OR BOTH AT THE SAME TIME!

Expert Tip: *The 4th Frame is an indirect strategy blending professional and personal elements, ideal for softening your approach when the 7-Step Close feels too direct or invasive in DMs. Use the 4th Frame to ease into the conversation, transitioning from indirect to direct as needed. AB test this spectrum alongside tweaks to your LinkedIn profile picture, banner, headline, about, and featured sections for optimal results.*

A/B Test Chat Flows*

A: 4th Frame = indirect
Try the lateral indirect approach to pulling to Zoom.

B: 7-Step = direct
Goals, goal behind the goal, what else have you tried, what's limiting you?

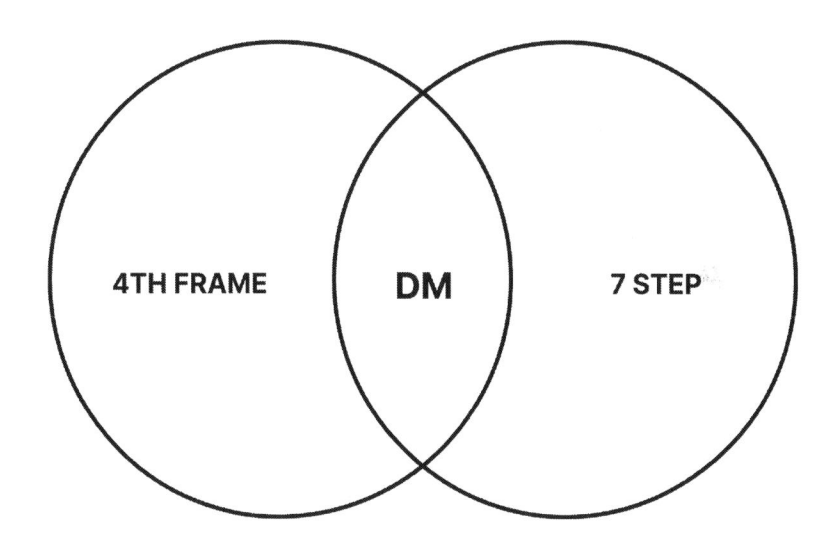

Sometimes, you can use the 4th Frame for DMs and the 7-step for full-cycle selling. Using both together is an advanced technique that requires experimentation and developing a "gut" feel.

Sliding into DMs is a battlefield because text loves turning harmless messages into passive-aggressive nightmares. "Hey, what time works for our meeting?" somehow reads like, "What time works for our meeting, Karen?!" It's so bad that HR now trains managers to use emojis—yes, emojis—to ward off drama. A well-placed smile emoji can literally save careers.

So, when you ask a bold or spicy question, soften it with emoji magic. Like, "Can you clarify this? 🦷" or "Hit that deadline yet? 🌶️" Big, bold questions? Great for Zoom. In DMs, they can hit like Darth Vader growling, "I find your lack of engagement disturbing." Emojis are the 2025 way of saying, "Relax, I'm not the Emperor." ⛈️

DM Sample Thread #1 - Team Lead:

Coach: how will you make Q3 better than Q2?
Prospect: well, we hired an outsourced agency to set appointments

Coach: that's interesting; what's your revenue goal?
Prospect: we need to hit $2MM at 4X pipeline

Coach: that makes sense. what have you tried to drive more pipe?
Prospect: doubling down on scripts we saw on the Gong webinar

Coach: have you ever worked with an executive coach? (shifting gears - going direct, setting a solid frame)
Prospect: we did have Johnny Mnemonic in here in the past

Coach: oh, that's great; how's that working out for you?
Prospect: good, but we've gotta build up our pipeline quickly now.

Coach: I'd love to connect and learn more about *you* if you're open to it.
–drop Calendly link–
(pull to Zoom)

It friggin' works like a hot knife through butter!

DM Sample Thread #2 - Individual Contributor (IC):
Coach: what's your big hairy goal for Q4?
Prospect: umm, well, I want to close 400K

Coach: OK, what's driving that?
Prospect: well, I need to pay off some debt

Coach: OK, what else have you tried: coaching, courses, training-wise?
Prospect: the company paid for Johnny Mnemonic, dug it

Coach: Oh, excellent, what do you think holds you back from hitting your goal
Prospect: my outbound *still* isn't working

Coach: OK, would you like some help with that?
Prospect: sure

Coach: I'd love to learn more about *you* if you're open to it – drop Calendly link –

One technique you'll see me using is sending testimonial screenshots or links to my book, reviews, a Substack article, and a Codex PDF right in the middle of a chat flow. I'll say, "How would you improve this guide?" Because opinions are like bad tattoos—everyone's got one, and most people can't wait to show it off—you'll get a 100% response rate.

Nail your "give." Something extraordinary, something you, yourself, would pay money for.

Humbly, even my free, open-source material became so valuable and ROI-producing that executives didn't want to share it because it was such a competitive advantage. Confession: I seriously considered not releasing this book, but my overwhelming desire to help millions of solopreneurs won.

What's your go-to "big name, big claim" for chats? Mine is: "Hey, I've helped reps 5X their income, or I've certified 65 reps at HubSpot that saw an average 4.6X increase in pipeline." Then, I'll drop this testimonial from Mike Milewski, BDR Leader at Skydio (repeat client champion):

> *"Most outbound leaders offer templates—'Do this, say that'—which helps. But when millions use the same scripts, they lose their edge. Worse, most reps don't understand WHY these templates work, so they can't create their own.*
>
> *Justin Michael is different.*
>
> *He gave me a million-dollar rod, taught me to catch the biggest fish, showed me how to build better rods, and connected me with other anglers to keep improving.*
>
> *Before Justin, I thought outbound didn't work in my industry. Four years later, my income has 4X'd, and I've never had more fun. Thank you, Justin—you've changed my life."*

"Real" Sample Thread #3 (booked meeting):

The opener was, "How will you make Q3 better than Q2?"

Prospect: Haha! Sorry about not getting back to you. This is our prime selling quarter, and things are lining up nicely for Q3.

JM: That's great. I appreciate your content. I would be honored if you read and reviewed any of my bestsellers. I was a VP, RVP,

GM, and in sales for 23 years. Now, I work with sellers to hit 500K/yr and launch side hustles. You may already be familiar with my work.

Prospect: Thank you; that's interesting. I'm not familiar with your work. No offense; I've just been pretty heads down the last five months. I am starting to come up for air, exploring opportunities to get me to the next level financially.

JM: That's great; I went from 45K to 2MM/yr building custom outbound systems. My passion is helping people create their best financial year ever. Without results, it's just pretty writing.

Prospect: So true! This has been my best year, but I haven't cracked 300K until now, at 46 years old. :-(

JM: Yeah, I plateaued for 15 years. Then, shot up to 750K, 1.2M, and 1.6M, finally crossing 2MM. My 3rd book reveals that 95% is a mindset and subconscious identity. That's not an indictment by any means.

Prospect: Fascinating, what a story. I'm working on that now and pinpointing which side hustle makes sense.

JM: Yes, with your acumen, you could hit 10K/mo in your sleep. I help people earn 20K/mo working only a few hours a week. I'm averaging $1,250 per hour despite lacking a college degree! Consulting is a goofy-foot surfboard to nail the acquisition, enrollment, breakthrough, and delivery pieces. Wall 1) Nobody wants coaching and consulting, and Wall 2) Nobody has money.

Prospect: There's opportunity cost, and I've done some advisory roles, but they haven't paid well.

JM: I'll help you solve Walls 1 and 2. Everyone wants you to bend over backward for equity. I'll ensure you get cash upfront. Here's my calendar:
(drop calendly)

Prospect: I'll find some time

"Real" Sample Thread #4 (booked meeting and closed)

JM: Hey, What's your big vision for 2025? Me? I've been helping coaches 2-5X their pipeline and income, as I built up to making over 2MM/yr coaching a few days a week. Worth exploring?

Prospect: Those are big numbers! I'm a little north of 10K/mo right now. I aim to double that by March 31 and triple it by mid-July.

JM: If you can see it in your mind, you can go there. What have you done to accelerate velocity? What was it like trading bonds? (*4th frame* personalization from his past jobs)

Prospect: I had excellent customers at Acme and did well with some of them, such as Beta and Zeta. But mostly, I was handed a book of business that was a churning blood bath! It was a huge learning experience to vet a product rather than using folks' words for the metrics, even if they were mentors.

To accelerate velocity, I've attended a few in-person events within my target market, led a workshop with a VC, and asked for network referrals.

JM: Would you like some help with that?
Prospect: Sure, let's connect.

DM Sample Thread #5 - Team Leader:

Coach: Do you think this whole ChatGPT messaging thing is overblown?
Prospect: What do you mean?

Coach: Well, are your reps getting meetings with ChatGPT sequences?
Prospect: Not really

Coach: What does your outbound motion look like?
Prospect: Well, you know, sporadic calling, some personalized sequences - it's standard, but we just don't see meetings like we used to

Coach: What are your goals for Q4?
Prospect: We need to hit 20 SQLs/rep/mo

Coach: OK, where are you now?
Prospect: Only 7

Coach: What's driving that goal?
Prospect: The CRO needs us at 5X pipeline so we can raise the next round. Board's putting pressure

Coach: Oh, that's interesting. What else have you tried to enable them?
Prospect: We just had a Johnny Mnemonic course, but it went OK - not quite enough uplift yet

Coach: OK, makes sense
I'd love to learn more about you if you're open to it.
(your Calendly link)

Do you notice how I *don't* shift gears here and ask, "Have you ever worked with an executive coach?" It's a team lead, VP to CRO, so I can safely assume he's qualified. Of course, they've used trainers in the past at funded companies.

Troubleshooting: Avoid "love bombing" — opt for muted acknowledgments instead. Saying things like, "That's amazing! Have you ever worked with a coach?" or "Wow, you're ahead of the game!" comes off as overly enthusiastic, making you seem needy, creepy, or salesy. Think of it like dating: showing too much "hunger" kills attraction. Instead, practice *Principled Disinterest* or the "Non-Hunger Theory" from *Combo Prospecting* by Tony J. Hughes (where I was a case study). Stay calm, confident, and curious.

Release your attachment to the outcome, and the desired result will naturally follow. It will always seem beyond your grasp when you cling to it out of need.

"Go pro," as Steven Pressfield says. True pros don't freak out. If someone ghosts after a back-and-forth DM volley, remember: where there's smoke, there's probably just them avoiding commitment like it's cardio. A little nudge to jog their memory can go a long way. Try something like, "Hey, remember when we were plotting to hit 400K? That wasn't just a dream sequence, was it?" Or, "Weren't we talking about obliterating that impostor syndrome and dialing up the self-esteem?"

Beware of permission-based openers (PBOs)—those low-status cold-calling relics like, "I know you're swamped" or "I must be bugging you." Dropping these in DMs is like handing them a mental Post-it note that reads, "Annoying telemarketer, 1995 vibes." Words like "busy" and "ugh" get stapled to your name forever. Think tone doesn't matter? Try inviting someone on a hot date to tour your "meth lab"—she'll ghost you faster than you can say, Walter White.

Instead, lean into positivity: "Hey, what if 2025 was the year you made that jaw-dropping transformation?" Or, "Let's talk about building your dream life – we'll call it Operation Win Big!" (NLP – neuro-linguistic programming – or as Belfort would call it, "future-casting"). Get them to picture their upgraded life on a high-def, cinematic level. And if they still drag their feet, don't hold back on a little reality check of what not changing could look like, aka sticking with the status quo. (Chandler)

A client keeps asking me every day: "Which sparks work?"

I'm like: "ALL of them!"

Warning: This section is the most popular part of what might be the most infamous chapter of any book I've written. Which is a *huge* flex! It's ballsy to suggest "sell by chat" is the new "cold calling." But here's the real risk: what happens when *everyone* slides into DMs with these chat flows? Will the *JMM* hit a saturation point, like Taki Moore's "Sell By Chat" did back when dinosaurs roamed the LinkedIn feed?

The answer? *Flank.* That's not just a military term; it's my secret weapon for linguistics and heuristics. If the world goes shortform *JMM*™, you go long-form. If everyone's doing George Clooney bumps, channel your inner Jack Nicholson—gritty, unpredictable, slightly unhinged. Zig while they zag. Heck, moonwalk if you need to.

This is why the *JMM*™ will outlast us all; OK, maybe not Cher and cockroaches. Look at what 99% of people are doing, then do the opposite. If the world goes left, you go right. If the world goes long, you go haiku. This strategy will still work when the year starts with "3." Because as long as people are predictable, you'll always have the upper hand. Or, as Jack would say, "You can't handle the truth!" But trust me, your prospects will.

Advanced Client Acquisition—Tips & Mindsets

A surefire way to snag clients? Join the ecosystem of a rival coach, swoop in for a guest spot, and drop some top-funnel wisdom. If that coach is focused on landing the big fish, congrats—you're now the yin to their yang, cross-selling into each other's networks like a boss. Shake & Bake! They'll teach *closing*; you'll teach *opening*. "Did we just become best friends? Yep!" (Any *Step Brothers* fans?)

Next move: borrow content like it's going out of style. Share a killer article or recommend a book—just make sure it's not yours. Chandler is the OG at this. It's simple: clients buy *you*. When you curate, add meaning, and explain *why* it's relevant, you become the go-to, not the author. Too many coaches clutch their IP like it's the last cookie, but the win is being seen as the trusted curator in their lives.

Pro Tip: Adopt the open-source mindset. Be the kind of person who can send clients to a Tony Robbins event without losing sleep (Byron Katie's probably next door anyway). Relationships—and business—thrive on trust. When you show trust, you get trust. Like Gordon "Sting" Sumner said: *If you love someone, set them free...* or at least let them explore other resources without losing your cool. Stop micromanaging your clients' journey—support their growth, even if some of it happens outside your ecosystem. That's how you build loyalty that lasts.

And now, the secret sauce to client acquisition: mastering the art of creating clients *anywhere*. Sitting next to you on a plane? Client. Standing by you in line at Starbucks? Client. People-watching at the DMV? Yes, even there. It's about training that radar to see potential, like scrolling a newsfeed or skimming a paper, and spotting a way to help. Inner Jedi intuition kicks in.

I'll often spot someone in my LinkedIn feed, track down their number, and hit them up on WhatsApp. Closed deals this way, believe it or not—that's how I met Christian Krause. He confirmed: "Yep, random Saturday morning cold call on WhatsApp." Sunday afternoon, Saturday morning—time zones blur, but the hustle is real.

I started messaging VPs: "What's your game plan to finish Q4 strong?" One replied, "Not into cookie-cutter approaches." I shot back, "Cookie-cutter? Me? No, but that's cute." He said, "Alright, let's chat." Boom—a 30-minute WhatsApp call compressed two weeks into one real-time close.

The trick? Stephen Covey's "speed to trust." It's the high-level, straight-to-the-point move. See a prospect online with their LinkedIn circle glowing bright green? Skip the wait; pull them into Zooms, FaceTime, SMS, or whatever it takes to get honest about the challenges and dreams they haven't even *admitted* to themselves yet. No one's got time to wait—so start future-proofing your pipeline *now*.

CHAPTER 7

Executive Targeting To Reach C-Level Clients & Build Coaching Funnels

"When something is meant for you, it will bring you peace and clarity, not chaos and confusion."

– Alex Elle

One of the sneakiest limiting beliefs new coaches cling to is this gem: *"I can only help people a few steps behind me."* False. Paradoxically, the higher up the ladder you go, the easier it gets! My first CRO client had me sweating bullets—I was questioning my existence. But within minutes, he grasped the *JMM* framework, taught it to his team, and rapidly added $2M to his pipeline. Senior leaders with insights? Like Viagra—hand them the goods, and they're up for anything.

Pro Tip: Follow the money. Target VPs, C-suite execs, board members, bestselling authors, and serial entrepreneurs. Worried your résumé isn't fancy enough? Doesn't matter. Solve their problem better and faster than they can, and they'll hire you. High-level clients respect your time, crave insights, and won't haggle over price. The result? Smooth engagements, big impact, and returns that make your bank account do a happy dance.

When chasing top-tier clients, here are a few hacks:

Tap the power nodes. Run a Sales Navigator search on connections of big names like Brendon Burchard or Aaron Ross. Overlap your networks, and boom—a second-degree goldmine.

- **Micro-file your case studies.** Shrink those glowing testimonials to under 100KB so they're ready to DM at a moment's notice. Small file, big leverage.
- **Let them write the curriculum.** Present a syllabus of your offerings and let them choose, like a menu. Coaching proposals should feel like the lease agreement for a $95K BMW—pages of itemized brilliance that scream, "This is worth every penny."

Mindset Hack: Act like they've already signed on at $500/hr or $5K/month. Coach as if they're already a client from the first call. What would you say? How would you deliver value? Start doing that now.

Steve Chandler nailed it: "Be real and tell them the truth about their problems." Translation: stop tiptoeing around and ask the bold questions:

- "What's the story behind your divorce?"
- "Tell me about losing your job."
- "Where are you suffering in life?"

It's intense, but this is *coaching*, not karaoke night. People don't need a cheerleader; they need someone brave enough to walk them through the fire. I once told a fractional CRO making $150K/year, "You don't need mindset coaching?

Really? Then why are you under-earning by six figures?" He hired me on the spot.

The fastest way to earn trust is by *breaking rapport*—strategically. Don't be a "yes coach." Spend 80% of the time encouraging and 20% challenging their worldview. Most clients block their growth with limiting beliefs they can't see. After coaching 1,000+ people, I can spot them in 30 seconds flat—and you'll develop that superpower, too. The real question is, are you bold enough to call it out? They'll love you for it—and you'll never run out of clients.

Troubleshooting:

Go too hard too soon, and you might snap the line. If you're delivering blunt truth bombs, use the Oreo technique:

1. Start with something nice.
2. Slide in the critique.
3. End with another positive.

For example: "Jane, your writing is brilliant, and you're fiercely independent. We need to work on your confidence in selling ROI—prospects will sense the hesitation. That said, your ability to synthesize ideas is top-tier." Like an Oreo: sweet, sharp, sweet. It protects their ego while driving home the truth.

Warning: Don't use this advice for evil. I had a client who thought being a cocky alpha was the way to go—negging prospects and flaunting his success like a bad dating coach. Sure, it worked short-term, but it left scorched earth, hurt feelings, and potential lawsuits in his wake. Coaching means *encouragement*. Period. If you don't respect your clients, they'll always feel it.

Final Word: Clients don't need fluff or feel-good vibes. They need bold, actionable truth. Be the coach who isn't afraid to shine a spotlight on their blind spots, and you'll transform their lives and build a business that feels effortless. Oh, and never pitch like a used-car salesman. Nobody trusts that guy.

The Coaching & Consulting Funnel–Breakthrough Required

I tackle limiting beliefs within the first 10 minutes of any session. Nail this skill, and you'll swim in clients faster than you can say "imposter syndrome."

"You don't think you're qualified to be a consultant?" Please—you've done more than I had when I started, and I've made millions. "Can't picture charging $500 an hour?" Look, people out there are charging that just to talk *about* charging that. You have a track record that blows seasoned coaches out of the water. Here's the deal: confidence in your value is like a magic wand for client trust and primo rates. Crack open that self-doubt, and clients will see you as their secret weapon, the coach they *literally* can't afford to miss.

Here's a real pep talk I gave a client:

"Listen, you're either making this happen or not. Fearless action wins—think jumping off buildings with a parachute you packed yourself. Training and coaching? It won't be on their priority list if *you* don't make it a priority for them."

Caution: Dealing with corporate types—VPs, CXOs, and CEOs—is like navigating a minefield of red tape and oversized egos. You can't just waltz in, drop a truth bomb, and tell them their baby's ugly. That's a one-way ticket to getting ejected faster than a crass political joke at an investor meeting. Instead, take the stealthy approach:

- Build them up.
- Listen to what's working.

- Nod at their successes like you're watching a TED Talk.

Once their guard is down, you can gently point out the gaps. Think scalpel, not sledgehammer.

And forget those epic two-hour coffee chats Rich Litvin used to rave about—ain't nobody got time for that anymore. Even he's pivoted to quick 20-minute calls because *time is your most valuable asset*. But here's the paradox: the slower you go, the bigger the payoff. Seriously. Go slower than a DMV line, and you'll close bigger deals.

Don't waste time with "tire kickers" fishing for free consulting. Trust your gut—it's like a spidey sense for time-wasters. You probably are if it feels like you're giving away too much. But also, don't dismiss potential gold. This balancing act becomes second nature after about 50 enrollment calls.

Here's my model: if you want seven figures in coaching, you can't just throw spaghetti at the wall. You *have* to create breakthroughs on the first call. Sometimes, with big deals, you'll need 2-3 disco calls before dropping your fees. But at some point—BAM—you hit them with:

"This might be the most money you've ever invested in yourself. But it could also be the turning point that transforms your life and creates a ridiculously abundant future."

Mic drop.

Alan Weiss is right: the more you slow down and invest upfront, the bigger the ultimate close. So, embrace the slow dance, my friends. Seven-figure coaching isn't a sprint—it's a waltz. Just don't step on anyone's toes, especially the CXOs. They *hate* that.

New Coaching Funnel - *JMM*:

1. Connect
2. Invite
3. Enroll / Create
4. Offer
5. Breakthrough
6. Close

Hat tip: Ryan Mathie and Rich Litvin for inspiration on this one.

CHAPTER 8

The First Close - 7 Steps to Zoom Call Glory

"Watch what everyone else does—then do the opposite. The majority is always wrong."

– Earl Nightingale

The mindset of "non-hunger," "principled disinterest," or, as I like to call it, "zero percent desperate vibes," is vital. When you're on a call, it's crucial to radiate that you don't *need* this business. It's the magic of a full pipeline—Kraig Kleeman nailed it when he said, "Pipeline cures all ills."

When you have more clients than you can shake a stick at, you can afford to be choosy, focusing only on those who align with your vision (and won't be a massive headache). That abundance? It's pure freedom. It's the credibility boost that says, "I don't need you, but if you'd like, I'm here to make you a success story."

The second a potential client smells even a whiff of neediness, they're out, or at best, on the fence. You could be following every tactic in this book like gospel, but the game's over if you come across as even slightly desperate.

The solution? Take on 5-15 clients at whatever rate you can get, coach them, and become "so good they can't ignore you." (Cal Newport / Steve Martin) Collect testimonials, referrals, and word-of-mouth buzz, and watch your rates skyrocket. This isn't just client acquisition—it's the way to go from "just a coach" to "*the* coach."

Without clients, coaches descend into the scarcity vortex—an endless spiral of insecurity, desperate LinkedIn posts, and rage-reading *The Subtle Art of Not Giving a F****. Stop the madness. Get The *50th Law* by 50 Cent and Robert Greene on your nightstand and ditch the people-pleasing. Not all clients are your people, and that's okay—you're not auditioning for *America's Got Talent*. The right ones will eventually line up, credit cards in hand, asking *you* for permission to work together.

Clients are like goldfish trapped in a jar—oblivious to the water they're swimming in. They see the symptoms (I need more leads, I can't find a niche), but you know the root cause (fear of being boring, rampant shiny object syndrome). You're the one with the flashlight, shining it into their cobweb-filled mental attic. They don't even know they need you—until you metaphorically hold up the mirror, and they go, "Oh crap, that's me?" (Credit to David C. Baker for this mic-drop analogy: "We can't read our own label from inside the jar.")

Before your first Zoom call, do some actual homework. Ask yourself, "How can I help this person?" Stalk them on Google like you're a private investigator, go forensic on their last ten LinkedIn posts, check their college major (Art History? Bold choice), and skim their recommendations for juicy tidbits. Don't come in cold like a telemarketer trying to sell life insurance at dinnertime. When you're genuinely curious, it shows. And that first impression? It's like a first date—except less awkward and without splitting the check.

"Beginnings matter..."

Speaking of beginnings, here's a gem from my own vault: A consultant once told me, "I'll only refer you if I can vet you on a call first." Challenge accepted. I unleashed my *7-step* close process, and by the end, they weren't just impressed—they were inspired. It turns out that they secretly wanted to start their own coaching business and hired my publisher to create a book series. Oh, and they wired me $12,000 by the following day. Moral of the story: Never underestimate the power of *pro-level coaching swagger*.

In a booming economy? Just double your rates. I once charged $10K/month, and a German CEO casually wired me $50K for five months of one-hour calls per week. Easiest money ever. Fun fact: Selling coaching is like selling a magic carpet—it's not about the rug; it's about the ride. Are you selling it like SaaS, though? That's a disaster waiting to happen. SaaS-style discovery calls for coaching are like trying to surf on a pool noodle—ridiculous, wobbly, and everyone's just pretending it's working.

Instead, disrupt the pattern. Stop with the BANT (budget-authority-need-timing) frameworks like it's 1999. Coaching is transformation, not transaction. So throw away the script, get them introspecting on their limiting beliefs, and watch the magic unfold.

Step 4 in my *7-step Close Process* is rooted in Scott Leese's *Addiction Model*: If people can't admit they have a problem, how will *they* ever change their behavior?

That's your job as a coach: to hold the mirror, hand them the flashlight, and—when needed—gently whack them with the metaphorical wake-up stick.

What's limiting you?

What's holding you back?

What's getting in the way?

What will happen if you don't change?

Why haven't you hit that goal yet?

How are you sabotaging yourself?

What are the lies you tell yourself about money?

When did you give up on your dream to ___fill in the blank___? (Chris Voss)

The first call isn't a cozy chat. As Steve Chandler would say, "Rent a shack by the river, hang a single light bulb from the ceiling, and go full Mossad interrogation on them."

Here's the problem: you're probably not landing clients because you're not going deep enough immediately. You're staying in the shallow end, and they're not trusting you enough to dive in. That's why I created this no-fail process to crack them open early. If you hit "The Money Convo" (a.k.a., The 2nd Wall) too soon, they haven't let you in yet.

Follow this playbook (below) to the letter on the first call, and you'll feel the polarity shift by step 4 when they finally admit their problem. That's the magic of the Scott Leese "Addiction Model." Steps 1-3 ease them enough that by step 4, they're ready to drop their guard and spill what's *really* going on.

Pressure test the first goal they give you; most people throw out fluff goals like "I just want more work-life balance." Uh-huh - as if that's a thing! It's your job to nudge them into seeing the bigger picture. Show them what their true North Star is and lock in. Get ready to help them think beyond their wildest corporate fantasies!

7 Steps to Closing So Smooth, It's Practically Hypnosis

1. **Find the Goal**

    Ask, "What's your goal?" It's almost always money, status, or revenge (*VP by June, Karen!*). If they get poetic about "balance," steer them back to the tangible stuff—like doubling income or crushing Q1.

2. **Unpack the *Real* Why**

    "What's behind that?" The goal isn't just about cash; it's about escaping debt, funding dream vacations, or winning arguments at Thanksgiving. Be a detective, not a yes-man.

3. **Clear Out the Baggage**

    "What else have you tried?" Cue the therapy session. Their past "solutions" are like bad exes—they need a controlled burn to make space for hope. And FYI, hope sells better than a free iPhone.

4. **Find the Blockers**

    "What's holding you back?" Translation: What's the excuse playlist running on repeat in their head? (Pro tip: Don't say, "It's you," even if it is. Just nod and look wise.)

5. **Share Your Messy Comeback**

    Tell your vulnerability story—how you flopped, learned, and crushed it. Everyone loves a good underdog-to-hero David Goggins story. Bonus: It makes you human and shows them transformation is possible.

6. **Flip the Script (Polarity Shift)**

   At this point, *they're* selling themselves to *you*. When they ask, "What's your fee?" try not to look too smug. If they don't, casually slide it in: "Want to know what working with me looks like?"

7. **End with Possibility, Not Price**

   When fees come up, keep the focus on their dream scenario—not sticker shock. "Imagine hitting [insert their big goal here]." Nobody wants to buy "affordable." They want transformation with a bow on it.

And just like that, you're closing deals and looking cool doing it.

Cracking the 7-Step Safe

This isn't just any safe—it's Fort Knox, and every step is non-negotiable. Skip step 2? Kaboom. Let them bait you into spilling your program or fees too soon? You're toast. This is a Michael Jackson-level choreography, not a freestyle dance-off. Stick to it. God gave you two ears and one mouth for a reason.

Discipline yourself to an 80/20 listen-to-talk ratio. Seriously, zip it and let them talk. You might be the first person ever to let them rant uninterrupted—and trust me, by the end, they'll practically convince themselves to sign up—no hard sell needed.

But the minute you go full "wah wah wah" Charlie Brown teacher, solving their problems and pitching your genius, they tune out, throw up a wall, and hit you with "send more info" or "I'll think about it." Trust comes from listening, not performing. Curiosity flips the switch—not your PowerPoint monologue.

I once had a coach so freaked out by this concept it was like watching someone try to sext with autocorrect on—awkward, disastrous, and absolutely not what anyone signed up for. Total meltdown: "But how will they know I'm amazing if I don't tell them every single thing I can do? Who's gonna give me $12,000 if I don't deliver a TED Talk about my genius?!"

Plot twist: it works the opposite way. *The best listeners close the most clients.* So, instead of turning your call into a one-man chainsaw juggling show, nod like a supportive bobblehead and let them spill. By the time they're done, they'll be sliding money your way faster than a drunk bachelor at a Vegas strip club.

7 Steps to Close (Remix): So Simple, It Fits on a Post-It

1. Their goal (no fluff, just ask).
2. The goal behind the goal (the juicy stuff).
3. What else have they tried? (their failure playlist).
4. What's holding them back? (make them squirm a bit).
5. Drop your story or a killer case study (plot twist vibes).
6. Polarity shift: make them *ask* for your fees.
7. Finally, pitch—but tie it all back to step 1, pure ROI, no filler.

I'm beating this dead horse again because the unlimited money glitch for DMs, meetings, and first calls deserves its own billboard. Stick to the script, or you'll look like someone trying to crack a safe with a spork.

Affordability vs. Possibility: The Deal Killer

The gravest mistake coaches make is ending a call talking about affordability, aka the kiss of death (hat tip, Chandler). That's why I hear clients whining, "They said they had to think about it." No, they don't. They're not sitting at home creating a Ben

Franklin-style pros-and-cons list about your coaching program. They're ghosting you.

This is why Step 7 is gospel: tie fees to ROI. Throw it back to Step 1—"What's your goal?"—because nobody stays up at night fantasizing about saving a few bucks. They're dreaming about tripling their income, getting promoted, or shutting up that smug coworker in accounting by suddenly splitting their time in Tuscany.

Remember! By minute 20, it's time to drop the "money conversation." Will they squirm? Probably. Will they grimace? Likely. But this is your moment to channel your inner therapist/coach hybrid. Hold space. Be the calm eye in the center of their storm of doubt. You're not here to pitch but to guide them into the cave they fear entering: investing in themselves. If you're not willing to lead them through it, who will? Gandalf? (News flash: it's you.)

If they hit you with, "What are your fees?" or "Can you walk me through your program?" do not, I repeat, DO NOT launch into logistics and turn into a human PowerPoint presentation. Nobody buys coaching because of cheat sheets, pre-recorded workshops, or Slack group access. Hit them with this instead:

"The program is *you*: your self-limiting beliefs, the lies you tell yourself about money, the way you hold yourself back. I'm the mirror that shows you what's missing and how to fix it." (Chandler paraphrasing).

If it's a team lead, tweak it to: "I'm here to identify where your reps are stuck and help them break through." Translation: I know what's wrong, and I can fix it.

This is where you remind them of the magic:

- We'll break through your limiting beliefs and self-sabotage.

- We'll uncover your unique zone of genius and monetize it fully. ("You're a razor with many blades; my job is to sharpen them all." Hat tip, Marylou Tyler)
- We'll combine my 24 years of experience with your expertise. ("1+1 doesn't equal 2—it equals 11." Thanks, Dad, for that math bomb.)

By this point, they're nodding so hard their neck hurts, and you've just opened the door to talk money.

When you get there, frame it like this: "My fees are designed to weed out the uncommitted. Imagine hiring a Navy SEAL for $200. Would you even bother waking up at 4 AM to meet them? My fees are an investment to make sure you're serious about your transformation."

Boom. They're not thinking, "How much does this cost?" They're thinking, "Am I ready to be Navy SEAL-level committed to my goals?"

Don't snooze on the follow-through when they say yes—and trust me, they will. This is where Steve Hardison's "event-action" rule comes in hot. Fire off that invoice *immediately*. Don't give them a second to overthink or suddenly decide they "need" that cash for a last-minute yoga retreat in Bali. Strike while the FOMO is fresh.

Oh, and yes, people crack up at the "You're fired" sign in my *3 Walls* diagram. They love to say, "Thanks, JM, you're fired," once they've squeezed every last drop of my wisdom. But let's be real—these same "I can't afford it" types magically "find" the cash for a neon-pink motorcycle with a sidecar for their dog the moment they want to. Coincidence? Please.

If all else fails and they still won't crack, channel your inner Shakespeare. Break the fourth wall and say: "I'm here to change your life. What do you want to change? What's not working? What's the opportunity you're afraid to seize?"

It's raw. It's uncomfortable. And it works. Because here's the truth: transformation isn't cheap—but staying stuck is a hell of a lot more expensive.

Landing the plane / effectively ending the first call:

"It's either a hell yes or hell no—there's no 'hell maybe.'" (Litvin). "Look, I get it. This is a big decision; I'm not here to pull some one-call-close jiu-jitsu move on you. Take your time. Go chat it over with your CEO, aka your significant other. I'll add you on WhatsApp and flood you with guides, testimonials, and real-life stories. Heck, I'll introduce you to some clients who'll tell you the good, the bad, and the 'Oh wow, that happened?' "

Then let those intros run wild. Don't hide from being back-channeled! You'll be shocked who advocates for you, sometimes even your worst enemy. I'll send 50+ testimonials and brazenly tell them to contact whomever they want. I've had some hilarious back-channel situations. Someone once just went rogue and texted Scott Leese—don't ask me why. Luckily, Scott had good things to say, and I closed the deal. Bitcoin transferred – just kidding! The industry's a tiny pond, so let your results be your PR team. And the screw-ups? Let them out, too; they'll find out faster than a Google search.

Bringing It All Together

Let's break it down—the *Justin Michael Method 3 Walls Model*™ in all its glory: a complete, unstoppable client acquisition system for solopreneurs designed to turn hesitant prospects into *hell-yes* clients. Here's how it works:

The 3 Walls

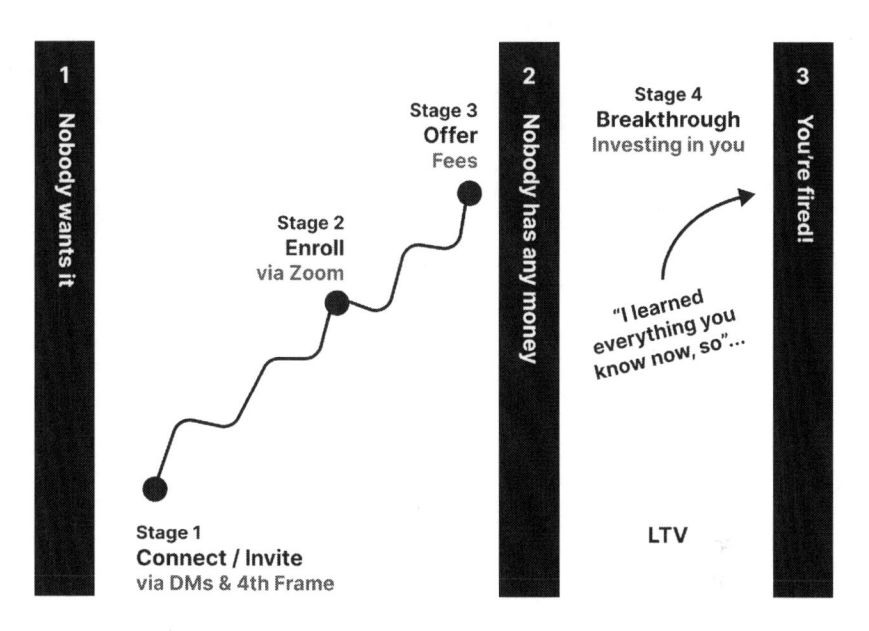

Diagram: Three vertical bars labeled "1 Nobody wants it", "2 Nobody has any money", "3 You're fired!" with a path showing Stage 1 Connect / Invite via DMs & 4th Frame → Stage 2 Enroll via Zoom → Stage 3 Offer Fees → Stage 4 Breakthrough Investing in you, with annotation "I learned everything you know now, so"... and LTV.

Phil Smith Design

1. The Connection and Invitation (DMs)

Start with the 4th Frame, "chat and grow rich," on LinkedIn. Spark curiosity and pull them onto Zoom. Easy.

2. The 7-Step Close (First Zoom Call)

Flip the script: build trust through vulnerability, shift polarity, and let them *sell themselves* on you. By the end, they're thinking, "I need this coach in my life." (Hat tip to gifted UK coach Matt Evans for inspiring the element of "seller vulnerability to cultivate buyer trust" inside the enrollment discussion.)

3. The Money Conversation (Minute 20)

Drop the fee around minute 20 of a 30-minute call or the 45-minute mark on a longer one. Proactively ask: "What comes up for you around the fee?" Stay present. Someone confides, "Johnny Mnemonic burned me for $18K." Respond: "Let's talk about that."

4. **The Breakthrough (Investing in you!)**

The "aha" moment hits. They're ready to sign, and you've guided them to it like a pro. Now, tie your fees to ROI. I'll say: "You lost $100K on bad coaches? I'll help you make a 5-15X return—plus that $100K back. Let's turn this into a redemption story." They laugh, but they get it. Coaching isn't a *cost*; it's a cash machine.

Money Objection Comebacks:

"I help clients generate $60K-$180K per year in additional income. If all we do is pay off my $12K fee, we've failed. My fees are a commitment to weed out the uncommitted. $5K/month, 3-month minimum commitment for a 5-15X return. It's either a hell yes or hell no—there's no hell maybe." (Chandler/Litvin inspo)

Not ready to commit on the spot? "Check with your CEO—aka significant other. Talk to my clients; they're my best closers."

Once the transfer clears, it's game on. I fire over a Calendly link so they can schedule ad hoc sessions as needed—none of that rigid weekly meeting nonsense. Why? Because I'm a firehose of tactics, and 90-minute calls tend to melt brains. This way, we cut the fluff and dive straight into action. My style? Think CrossFit for human performance, minus the chalk dust and occasional ego bruises.

And yes, I'm not afraid to assign homework—*every single time*. But relax, I'm not here to bury you under a pile of books (even though I *could* because, hello, prolific author here). Instead, my motto is simple: Be awesome and actually do the stuff you paid for. This isn't a dress rehearsal, people. No crying in baseball. No free rides in *Waterworld*. And absolutely no refunds from the Karma Bank if you don't show up. So strap in and go crush it.

Oh, and just so you know, I've had siblings sign up together faster than you can say "Winklevoss Twins." My work? It's that good. And… I'm humble!

Pro Tip (and mildly hilarious side note): Never stick a form fill or questionnaire on your calendar. You want to create some *pull*, some *mystery*, a little "What's this wizard going to teach me?" vibe so they appear curious. I swear, I had a client who would solve *all* their clients' problems within five minutes. Hold something back! Let them have some "a-ha" moments. If you blow their mind in the DMs or during the first five minutes of the call, why bother meeting?

Qualifying clients with endless forms is like hosting a dinner party and making guests fill out a five-page menu—zero intrigue! One client's seven-step form screamed $99 gym membership, not $25K coaching. High-end coaching should feel like a chef's tasting menu: exclusive, effortless, and full of surprises.

Meanwhile, some "11X" trainers out there will pull *any* trick to close a sale, advocating used-car-lot tactics that make you feel like you need a shower. Here's my approach: "catch and release." Be willing to walk away. Trust me—nothing's more attractive than not *needing* them. They'll be drawn to you like cats to an empty box.

And here's the follow-up trick: after the call, don't rush, push, or hound them. Give them space. Then, slide back into their DMs a day or two later with some real value (and no "just checking in" snooze fest). Try: "Here's a quote that reminded me of our convo," or, "Check out this Substack article I wrote." You could even throw them a link to a talk by Neville Goddard, David Bayer, or Kathleen Cameron. Keep it classy; keep it cool.

Now, about fees: upfront payments only! Why? Because without skin in the game, you'll end up in your own personal *Jerry Maguire* sequel, begging clients to "Help me help you!" I've seen people drop $2.5K, then disappear faster than Jerry's clients after his memo, mumbling excuses like, "Your vibe shifted, bro!" Spoiler alert: it's not the vibe; it's their wallet. Stick to "Show me the money!"—Jerry would approve.

Here's a sample talk track on fees to keep things clean: "One-off fees: $5K for two hours, $10K for a month. Commit to three months? I'll do $5K a month. Pay upfront for 3-6 months, and I'll shave off 20-30%." My minimum used to be $30K for three months in the bull market, with 20% off upfront. Then, when the recession hit, I cut it in half. As Ankush Jain, Rich Litvin, and Steve Chandler (probably) say, "Coach your butt off until you're *so good they can't ignore you*. Then you'll grow by referrals and invites *only*."

ABC: Always Be Coaching. How do you become a master coach? Coach like your life depends on it day and night.

Once they're in, joke, "You should talk to Ron—he'll give you the good, the bad, and the ugly, like a one-star Yelp review written in all caps." Transparency is your best friend. Never take yourself too seriously—self-deprecating wit is the secret handshake of real leaders.

Want to level up? Put your client's interests first. I even refer them to other coaches—yep, I send people off to masters like Jamal Reimer, Ankush Jain, John Patrick Morgan, Rich Habets, and Townsend Wardlaw all the time. Far from losing them, you inspire loyalty. It's the ultimate paradox.

De-Niching–From Pitching to North Star

Most folks chant "nail your niche" or preach "the riches are in the niches" like it's the 11th commandment. I say, scrap the gospel and light that rulebook on fire. Why squeeze yourself into a tiny vertical box when you can go horizontal and build a coaching pipeline that explodes like a soda can launched off a rooftop?

Here's the play: flip your niche on its side and let it spread out like an all-you-can-eat Vegas buffet. No more starving for scraps in some narrow lane—picture a horizontal beast of a market that scoops up demand from everywhere. Imagine a sad, skinny vertical line in your diagram suddenly transforming into a horizontal juggernaut of opportunity. The result? A bigger, juicier market that doesn't just feed growth—it force-feeds it. And who doesn't love a little prime rib with linguini at 7 am?

DE-NICHING

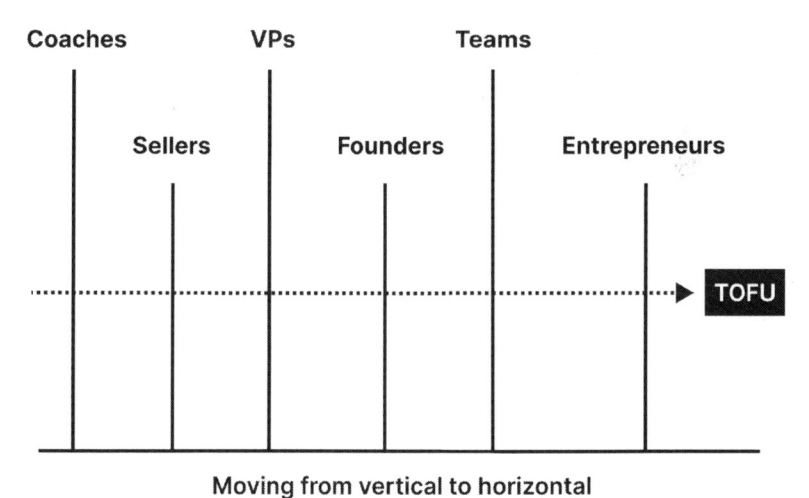

Moving from vertical to horizontal

TOFU = top of funnel

I started as "Salesborg," slapping the Terminator on my face in what Jeremy Donovan called a CLM—career-limiting move—and tag-teaming with Aaron Ross in *Sales Trainer WrestleMania*. Back then, I was babysitting baby sellers, teaching them to stop crying, pick up the phone, and close a deal without needing a juice box.

Now? I coach leaders with a pulse (and a few who are just really good at pretending). I've worked with the heir to a Costco hat dynasty (because *that's* the crown jewel of capitalism), the emperor of a real estate coaching empire (even emperors need a nudge), and a conflict resolution expert from Google (*irony sold separately*). Turns out, Salesborg doesn't just tolerate humans—he even finds them *mildly entertaining* on occasion.

Here's the deal: if you niche down too far, you'll end up eating ramen and explaining to your kids why dessert is just air tonight.

The secret? Stop treating your "ideal client" like an impossible mission to decode enemy intel—this isn't James Bond, and your client isn't hiding in a villain's lair. Focus on the human in front of you. Call out their blind spots, obliterate their "woe is me" mindset, and upgrade them into a self-empowered rockstar. Say "custom" and "bespoke" so much it could be a drinking game. Why? Because people pay for personal. Think sweaty Zumba class vs. a Jocko Willink Navy SEAL experience dragging you up a mountain 1:1. Which one screams premium?

Wrap it all in a logistics container (yes, I know, it sounds like IKEA for business). Offer flexibility, ad hoc access, and a clear plan: "We meet twice weekly, unlimited chat, async support—what's our first mission?" Boom. Now you've got a high-touch program that screams exclusivity and slaps a big, fat price tag on itself.

So, how do we *de-niche*?

Forget "Greg, the disgruntled CFO with action figures." That's like designing a roller coaster for one guy—what's the point? Focus on the fireworks: results so dazzling they make clients feel like they're front row for a Fourth of July finale. Nail this, and clients will swarm like kids chasing churros.

Leap across industries like you're park-hopping between Disneyland and Magic Mountain—fast, fearless, and too busy creating magic to care about job titles. Just don't water down your genius into theme park nachos—functional, but nobody's lining up for it. You're going from niche to Disneyland: a must-see attraction for everyone without losing your magic. Flaunt your wins like a parade float, collect success stories like souvenir mugs, and soon your business will run like Space Mountain—wild, thrilling, and leaving everyone screaming, "Again!"

SECTION III

Sealing the Deal & Scaling Up

*"Your attitude, not your aptitude,
will determine your altitude."*

– Zig Ziglar

CHAPTER 9

Premium Enrollment - Command Top Dollar & Own the Money Talk

"The fishing is best where the fewest go and the collective insecurity of the world makes it easy for people to hit home runs while everyone else is aiming for base hits."

— Tim Ferriss.

In 2006, Jack Canfield dropped a game-changer on me: the power of making *big, bold asks*, inspired by *The Aladdin Factor*. His advice was simple yet brilliant: "Why are you afraid to ASK ultra-high-net-worth (UHNW) individuals if you can help them or their business?" It's a classic, irrational, limiting belief. Sure, they might have a yacht, a mansion, and an honorary PhD in Being Ridiculously Impressive—but here's the kicker: UHNW clients are often the easiest to close and the most rewarding to serve.

I wondered where on Earth I'd find "these people." Then, the other day, an advisor jumped on the phone, casually dropped that he'd just exited a company, driven his second Ferrari home, and had a meeting with Peter Thiel coming up. There he was, right out of an episode of *Rich People Problems*. He'd found me through a second-degree LinkedIn spear, read my books, and is now working with me to craft an outbound strategy for a next-gen AI customer service simulator. This happens when you make those big asks—your ideal clients pop out of the woodwork like they were just waiting for you to appear.

My dad used to tell me, "Think bigger!" He also said I was "the most fearless person he knew with, and I quote, 'balls the size of mountaintops.'" Can I print that? Eh, I just did.

The point is: How do you know you *can't* help someone if you don't even *ask*?

We all have the same 24 hours. All we control is how hard we swing the ax. Fortune favors the bold, so go big. Instead of a generic ask, laser-focus on an insight they've never heard. Hold people accountable for beliefs they've never questioned. Dig for what truly drives them. As Litvin says, "Find their secret dream."

Here's the deal: closing a $25K/month client isn't all that different from closing a $3K/month client. But my rule for fees? If you charge too little, you resent the client; if you charge too much, they *own* you. My $25K/month client set me up like a Fractional VP and ran me ragged with seven Zoom calls a week, usually about product marketing (help!).

Anchor every deal with a high-fee offer, like six months of 1:1 consulting. Then, down-sell into a group or cohort if needed. It's like a BMW dealership: you walk in drooling over the $150K M5, and before you know it, you're leasing a 3-Series for $500/month. BMW's a genius bank with wheels—3, 5, 7, 9. Your group offering can be the gateway drug to your 1:1 work, but remember, these are often two different audiences.

Coaches often start clients in low-fee cohorts and then wonder why they're not upgrading. Anchor high, down-sell if necessary, but don't box yourself into the bargain basement.

And here's a pro tip: If you offer someone $12K for 1:1 and they have $4,500, take the $4,500 and customize a mini-plan. $15K from five $3K clients beats the heck out of 0% of 0.

Above all, keep that confidence dialed up to eleven. Clients can sense even a microgram of self-doubt. Cultivate unwavering belief in yourself, your skills, and the infinite universe rooting for you to succeed.

Embrace pronoia: "The universe is plotting to do you good!"

Thoughts are things. If your brain's running a steady loop of doubt, worry, and overwhelm, congratulations—you've sunk your ship before it even left the dock. Want unshakeable confidence and belief? Read *Attraction Selling (JMM 3.0)* and stop sabotaging yourself before your first cup of coffee.

Here's the deal: the number one reason to stay positive isn't just to feel good—it's because you're modeling that mindset for your clients *and* yourself. You're literally selling belief. If you want to inspire change, you have to *be* the change. (Nelson Mandela said it first, but we'll roll with it.)

Now, if you're out here trying to build a coaching empire while secretly resenting your clients' success or getting competitive with them, you've got some soul-searching to do. David Bayer calls it a "Resentment Audit."

Step 1: Write down everyone you resent like you're making a hit list, but less murdery.

Step 2: Forgive them like you're Oprah on her *Favorite Things* episode—"And YOU get forgiveness! And YOU get forgiveness!"

Step 3: Take it up a notch: hype them up, send them good vibes, and genuinely wish for their success like you're their personal cheerleader. Pom-poms optional.

Why? Because jealousy is the silent killer of connection. You can't genuinely help someone while low-key hoping they trip on their way to success. Let it go. Their wins don't take away from yours—if anything, they fuel your credibility. So, get excited about their happiness and prosperity. Your brain, your clients, and your business will thank you.

Franky said it best, "The best revenge is massive success."

Real coaching conversation: Case study turning around mindset, powerful client realizations:

> "It's been a roller coaster this week, but I learned a lot.
>
> #1 You have to sleep and take care of your health.
>
> #2 Deals closed are a lagging indicator of effort.
>
> #3 I will build a 600k-a-year coaching business in 2025.
>
> #4 People need my help, and the market has a massive skills gap.
>
> #5 I need to be more consistent with my prospecting."

My response (real dialog/pep talk):

JM: All you can do is act and have faith. You could take all these actions and doubt yourself and have limited success. You could take the same actions with *unshakeable* belief and kill it. Kathleen Cameron had a Network Marketing business where she made the same number of cold calls daily and shifted into a positive self-identity, knowing she'd attract clients. Suddenly, her success rate shot up, but the kicker was that she wasn't *doing* anything differently. She just changed her attitude. It's quantum mechanics; how we *perceive* the world impacts the outcome.

CLIENT: Is there anything wrong with dropping all my fear and anxiety about it, not working out, relaxing, and trusting God while also taking massive action? All the worry and fear are exhausting, and none of these worst-case scenarios I have in my head are materializing; it's the opposite.

JM: When you were a top AE, did you live in constant worry and fear?

CLIENT: No, not at all. It was the opposite.

JM: So why make this mistake now? I say this with love. Optimism and positivity will allow you to grow. How can you believe you'd crush AE and fail as a coach? Enterprise software sales is 10 times harder, IMHO. Quiet your mind and realize this job is way easier. Logically, think about it; this was my calculus.

Watch some lectures by Syd Banks. There is only Mind, Consciousness & Thought. *The 3 Principles.* Per Michael Neill, 'we are living in the feeling of our thinking.' Every fear, doubt, and worry is a thought. You are not your thoughts. YOU *think* your thoughts. The *real* you! You are the infinite awareness behind it all.

CLIENT: Amazing!

JM: Don't believe in negative thoughts; they are lies that don't exist, just patterns from trauma.

CLIENT: You are right

JM: We have 70K thoughts per day. 80% of our thoughts are harmful, and 95% are repetitive (National Science Foundation). The same goes for Michael Jordan, Oprah Winfrey, and Richard Branson; we are all hard-wired, instinctive human animals with a protectionist lizard brain.

So, *believe* in positive affirmations. Dwell on your testimonials. Dwell on your past accomplishments. Nobody can take them away from you. Have faith, and potential clients will *sense* all this. They'll feel it if you operate with hidden fear and doubt.

Remember, from a change in *being*, your thinking and doing change eternally.

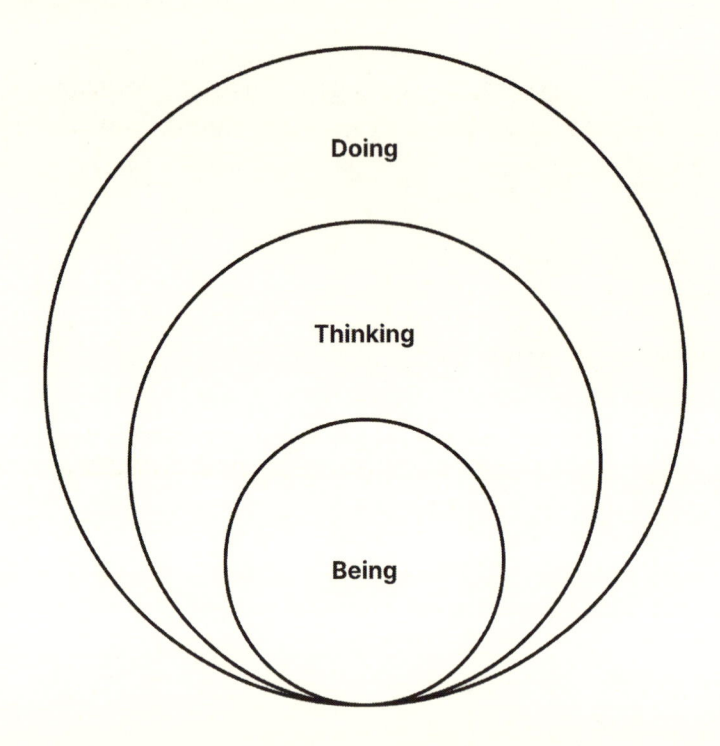

My coaching superpower? It's an ironclad, unshakable belief in myself that borders on ridiculous. I'm talking full-on, 24/7, "I'm my own hype man" levels of confidence. Bold moves, all day, every day. Zero self-doubt. Not even a *whiff* of hesitation. That's how you build an empire from thin air—the laser focus of a tiger mixed with the unquestioning optimism of a golden retriever chasing a tennis ball.

If you're not sold on yourself, your clients won't be either. You need to love yourself like your own No. 1 fan and believe in yourself 1000%, or you'll be pushing that boulder up a hill like Sisyphus forever. Self-doubt? Not in this dojo. If you can't hype yourself up, how can you expect to transfer that belief to clients? They'll sense any wobble in your confidence, like a shark smelling blood in the water.

Believe in your results, your client's results, and every bit of untapped potential hiding inside them. See the gold in them. Show them the gold in them. They'll feel it—and that's when the magic happens.

Enrollment Power–Status Dynamics & Frame Control

One-call closing is not the goal, although I often do serendipitously.

I wrap up most calls with a takeaway, usually by talking the client *out* of working with me. I love the Hormozi classic to pressure test the deal, "Why wouldn't you move forward?" Or:

"Ed, I know this is a big decision. Let's not lock this down on a single call. Why don't you chat with your CEO, spouse, psychic—whoever you run big life decisions by? Get real talk from my clients on the good, the bad, and the awkward. We'll circle back next week."

And if all you get from that first or second meeting is a request for a proposal? That's a win! As Alan Weiss says, "The more you frontload the relationship, the bigger the close." Translation: slow and steady brings the payday.

"Enrolling" isn't a sleazy sales move—it's a vibe. It's about creating an energy so magnetic they can't resist leaning in. Enrollment doesn't push, defend, or go into a hostage negotiation parody. It's just you, genuine and compelling, without trying too hard. When you take this "enrolling" approach, you're not selling—you're attracting clients like they're drawn to your gravitational pull.

Sandler and Costanza's genius? "Do the opposite." So when I'm onboarding a client, I go right for the heat. I'll ask, "What concerns do you have? What's holding you back? What's the thing you're *not* saying?" And if I'm making a referral, I'll say, "Ask Aaron what he didn't like, OK?" Being a trustworthy advisor means offering the "full monty" 360-degree experience—warts and all.

Leaning into the awkward stuff—the fee, their budget, their motivation (or lack thereof)—builds more trust than the "used car lot" vibe. None of that "smile and nod, tell them what they want to hear" nonsense. Carolyn Freyer-Jones calls it out in her books: show up as your *professional* self, not the people-pleasing "social self" desperate for a pat on the head.

One of my favorite hard asks? "Billy, so…when am I coaching you? " Bold, right? And the best response I got? Not a brush-off. Instead: "I'm saving up to afford you."

"Hard closing" is like proposing on the first date—awkward, desperate, and sure to end with someone sneaking out the bathroom window. Let's keep it cool. Instead, think of it as *catch-and-release fishing*. End the call with something smooth like, "I know this is a big decision. Take your time, think about it, and feel free to chat with my clients." Then reel them back in with a follow-up the next day: "What's been on your mind since we spoke?" Offer a second call to tackle their hesitations, help them refocus on their dream, and—if needed—MacGyver a way to find the money.

"The greatest fear in the world is of the opinions of others. And the moment you are unafraid of the crowd, you are no longer a sheep; you become a lion. A great roar arises in your heart, the roar of freedom." – Rajneesh (Osho). (Translation: stop being a sheep.)

Coaching exists because people are stuck on their personal *Island of Frustration*, surrounded by sharks, seaweed, and saltwater, making them grumpy. Your job? Be their boat to the *Island of Awesomeness*, brimming with fresh coconuts, a protective reef, and stellar WiFi. Carolyn Freyer-Jones calls it *The Island Metaphor*. Ask them: *"What's on your dream island? Paint me a picture."* Then drop this magic phrase: "What's getting in the way?"—because there's always something lurking in the water.

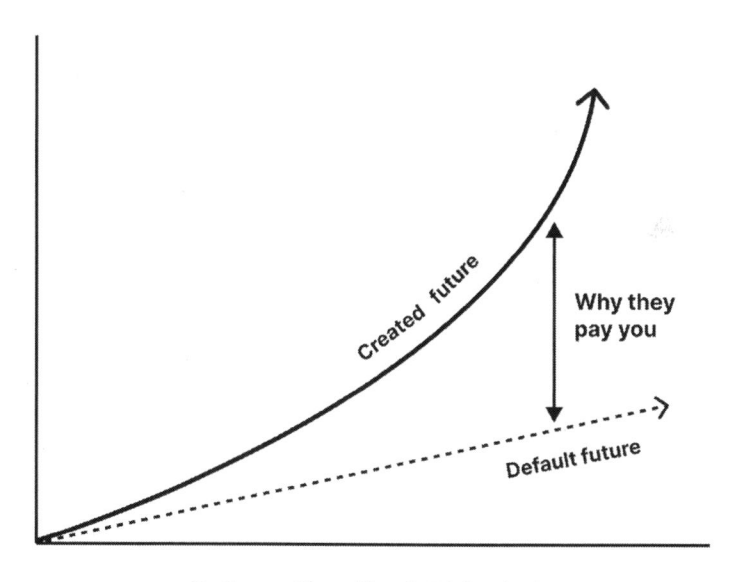

© *Steve Chandler & Rich Litvin*

> *"Create your future from your future, not your past."*
>
> *— Werner Erhard*

Why do they pay you? Rich Litvin nails it: They pay because they're confident you've delivered results for people just like them. It's not about how many IPOs you've exited or the fancy coaching certificate you laminated at Kinko's print shop. They hire you because you've transformed yourself and helped others cross the same chasm they're staring at. You've moved them from their default future to a *created* one á la Werner Erhard, which is absolutely priceless, my friends.

Tell them stories. "I had a client just like you. Here's where they started, and here's where they ended up. Ask them about it!" Transparency is sexy—and *enrolling*. Don't hide your backchannel; make all your clients referenceable. If they trust your track record, they'll believe you're the boat that gets them where they need to go: sharks and all.

Bank up a stash of testimonial screenshots and videos like your life depends on it. If you're just starting, coach some friends for free or at a discount. Don't worry—they'll pay you back in glowing reviews.

> **"Had two sessions with Justin and closed $7K already."**
>
> *— Donie*

See? Proof sells.

Now, let's talk about *status*. As the coach, you *must* hold the more powerful frame. Why? Because the second you let the balance slip, the roles reverse, and suddenly, they're coaching *you*. It's like dating—don't let them put you in the friend zone (FZ).

"Do you want to have a chat?" they ask.

"I don't do chats," you reply. "I charge $2,000/hr, but I'm happy to invest some time brainstorming how to double your income by 2025. No hard sell." Then you drop the Zoom link like a boss.

Sure, you can give away the first call as a complimentary session, but set the tone: "This is an experience of my coaching, not free consulting." If they say, "I'm broke," you decide if a 20-minute coffee chat is worth your time—or if they're just window-shopping for free advice.

Stay out of *wishy-washy networking limbo*. Phrases like "Let's just network and see what happens" are code for "I'm going to waste your time with free consulting and vague promises." Make your intentions clear from the start: "I'm the coach. You're the client I want to help. Let's get to work." That's holding the frame.

And yes, you're going to get ghosted. Clients will give you a verbal green light, only to vanish like they're starring in a David Copperfield magic act. If you catch them live, ask, "What's getting in the way?" Offer to book another call to dive deeper into their challenges and remind them of the dream.

Here's the play: Reorient them to their vision, the second island, the land of WiFi and fresh coconuts. Keep their focus on value, ROI, and social proof until the "pain of staying the same" outweighs the "pain of change" (Brent Adamson). Sell the dream, not the price tag. Keep them living in possibility, not affordability, because nobody gets inspired by a discount code.

Top 11 Ways to Enroll Clients Without Sounding Like a Pushy Salesbot from Planet Close-Itron
(heart of this book & method!)

1. **No hard closing (Soft sell vs. hard sell)**

   Think of it like a first date: no one whips out a prenup over appetizers. Let it breathe.

2. **Catch and release (be willing to walk away)**

   Be like a cool cat with a toy mouse. Bat it around a bit, then walk away. They'll come chasing.

3. **Slow down to speed up**

   Don't floor it. This is more of a Sunday drive and less NASCAR. Let them *want* to accelerate.

4. **Leverage testimonials and reference clients**

   It's like saying, "Don't take *my* word for it; ask the fan club." They're not hiring you just for your charm—they need proof.

5. **Give them the breakthrough, which is hiring you**

   Sometimes, their greatest lightbulb moment is realizing they're investing in themselves. You're the Coach Everest of their financial decisions.

6. **"The cave they fear to enter contains the treasure they seek!"**

   (Hat tip: Joseph Campbell and Paulo Coelho) Translation: that scary investment? Yeah, that's where the magic happens.

7. **Other orientation and deep listening (it's all about them!)**

   Put the jazz hands down. Pulling an Anchorman with a flaming jazz flute? Awkward, unnecessary, and nobody asked. Chill—humble beats Rolex every time.

8. **Vulnerability = trust = polarity shift**

   Show a crack in that polished exterior; it's like giving them a key to the inner circle.

9. **Get creative in finding the money**

   Who says the money has to be in their *bank account*? Get scrappy. There's always a way.

10. **There are no "nos"—only boomerangs**

    A "no" is just a client taking the scenic route. They'll be back. Trust.

11. **Who you are attracts clients**

    Confidence isn't loud. It's that quiet, "I've got this" vibe that says you're the alpha leader they've been waiting for.

"The best investment you can make is in yourself."

– *Warren Buffett*

Mastering the Money Talk–Breaking the 2nd Wall

She smiled and asked, "So, how do I pay you?" I nearly high-fived myself. This could be you soon—let's get you there.

Too many coaches hear the slightest hesitation from a client and buckle. The client winces, and suddenly, you're offering a discount like you're running a clearance sale. Resist the urge! Instead, ask, "What's coming up for you around the fee?" If they say, "I can't afford it," don't drop the price—dig in. "Ever invested in something like this before?" Maybe they'll go, "Yeah, I spent $25K on mindset coaching, and it didn't work." That's your opening. "Oof, that sounds frustrating." Clear the old disappointment so they can leave their "default future" (a.k.a. "stuckville") behind and step into the breakthrough they *actually* want.

Remember, they're investing in *themselves*—often more than they've ever spent on anything other than a car or a kitchen remodel. Are they crossing that investment threshold? That's where the magic happens. And you're the coach who got them there.

Whenever they ask your fee, don't just blurt it out like you're selling a sandwich. That's rookie stuff. Try this layer cake flow instead:

1) Methodology >> 2) Logistics >> 3) Fees tied to ROI

Throw in, "Want me to walk you through how I work?" Make sure they get it. Then, ease into the logistics. Finally, hit them with the fees but close on that sweet 5-15X return. Let the results speak louder than the sticker shock.

Money objections

I will say, "If it takes 9 months to pay off my 12K or 15K, that's a huge fail. My reputation is damaged. I want this to be the turning point in your life. I want you to look back in 2026 and say, 'Oh snap, this Justin Michael guy in the funny animal hat is *why* I earned 200K more, even millions more, toward 2030.' Otherwise, what are we doing here? Let's not waste each other's time."

Troubleshooting the Money Conversation

If money's the hurdle, you've got two choices: go after clients with deep pockets or get crafty with payments. When in doubt, suggest some unconventional "funding strategies:" credit cards, loans, or even a friendly call to Aunt Edna for a little "personal growth sponsorship." Only about 5% of clients can drop big bucks without blinking (the top 5% of Americans make $335,891). But there's often inheritance, family cash, or a mysterious box of old coins somewhere. As long as you deliver results, it's all fair game!

I once had a minor league baseball player making $35K wire me $15,000 for coaching because he was thrown into an SDR leadership role and needed immediate help not to flop. When people truly feel the need, they find the funds—without pain or urgency, there's no sale. I've seen clients cash out Google stock, Bitcoin, and even unexpected estate payouts. I didn't chase this—they got resourceful.

97% of my clients crush it and get their investment back. The other 3%? They either ghost halfway through or think "manifestation" means sipping Mai Tais and scrapbooking.

And then there's *The Cutting Board Caper*. This guy starts mailing everyone oak cheeseboards with notes like, "Can we carve out some time?" It was effective! Two weeks in, I ask, "How's *JMM* going?" He says, "I haven't started, but I don't think it works." Then he pans the camera to a mountain of cutting boards and stamps, licking one for good measure. I nearly fell out of my chair.

The point is that people will get creative if they're serious about working with you. You might need to help them brainstorm a bit. Ask them about their budget if they can't afford the full $12K.

"Can you swing $4K?" If they say yes, you can start with a limited scope. Or give them the nudge: "Great, wire that by Friday, and we'll make it happen."

When they're invested, you'll see them shift their budgets, reprioritize, and become resourceful. Think back to your last 50 prospects who didn't buy. Was it the cash, or did you just miss the chance to dig into their pain to create urgency? The money's out there—sometimes it's just hiding behind a stack of fancy cheeseboards.

Money Checklist: Why They Didn't Pay You (and How to Fix It)

1. **You didn't unlock their secret dream.**

    If you can't make them picture their dream life like it's a *Hallmark movie montage*, they're not pulling out their wallet. You need to be the Nicholas Sparks of coaching pitches.

2. **They didn't trust you enough.**

    No trust = no money. They need to see you as the Gandalf of their journey, not some random vagrant yelling, "You shall not pass unless you Venmo me $5K!"

3. **You bailed on the money topic too early.**

    If you got nervous and moved on, congrats—you left money on the table. Hold the space, keep your cool, and coach them through their money hang-ups like a zen master.

4. **You didn't get creative about funding.**

    Savings? Credit cards? Uncle Joe's emergency "buy-a-boat" fund? Selling Bitcoin? If they want it bad enough, there's always a way. Be their co-conspirator in figuring it out.

5. **You didn't create enough desire.**

   If you crank up their desire high enough, they'll move mountains—and max out credit cards—to work with you. Desire trumps budget every time.

6. **Everyone has a credit card.**

   No, seriously. Even your grandma has one stashed "just in case." Maybe it's time for you to roll out a *Manifesting for Boomers* program.

7. **You didn't ask for a partial payment today.**

   Get some skin in the game! Take $500, $1,000—whatever they can do now—and scope the delivery. Five $3K deals in a week is $15K. You don't need one big deal; you need *momentum*.

8. **You ignored their significant other's influence.**

   Budget decisions are a team sport for most couples. Offer to get their partner on the call. You're not just coaching the client—you're coaching the *unit*.

9. **They're in transition, and you didn't coach them up.**

   If they're between jobs, don't write them off. Help them land the next gig so they can afford you. I wholeheartedly recommend *60 Seconds, and You're Hired* by Robin Ryan.

Coach them, connect them, and introduce them to your network. Before you know it, you'll be the career mafia don—people whisper your name in hushed tones, and everyone owes you a favor they can't refuse.

Pro Tip: Be the coach who's so helpful they'd sell their Peloton to pay you.

No matter who you target, buyers are liars—it's a universal truth. Everyone guards their bank accounts like dragons hoarding gold. Whether they're making $400K with years of GTM experience or just starting out, your job is to slow down, coach them around the money, and grease the payment wheels. Get paid upfront for mutual skin in the game. Once they invest, they'll magically become 100 times more accountable.

Troubleshooting: The Money Conversation

If you struggle to close, take the temperature early on the first call. If they're playing coy, try these:

- "You got on this call for a reason; what's *really* going on in your life?"
- "Why would you talk to a coach if there's nothing you want to change?"

When they hit you with "I don't have the money," respond:

- "What comes up for you around the fee?"
- "Have you been burned before?" (Hint: the answer is always *yes*.)
- "The average American has 3.84 credit cards—can you put it on one?"
- "How can we get creative to find the money?" (Family loans? Bitcoin? Selling the Beanie Babies Collection?)

If they say, "It's too expensive," ask: "Relative to what? What if the ROI is 5-15X? Talk to my client Scott about his results."

I'll stay on this for 5-10 minutes, metering it carefully—minute 20 in a short call, minute 45 in a longer one. Timing matters.

Creative Payment Sources
Business loans, credit cards, family, stock, inheritance, Bitcoin—if they want it bad enough, they'll find it.

Caveat: Ethics Matter
If you can't drive ROI, don't go after these sources. As Townsend Wardlaw says, "If you can't deliver ROI, you're not ready to be a true business coach." Aim for at least a 3X return or help them land a solid job first if they're in transition. Alan Weiss's *Hippocratic Oath for Consultants* applies: "Do no harm."

Time Objections
When they say, "I don't have time," reframe it: "Then do it for your family—your anchor. Showing up for yourself is showing up for them." Or simplify with an abridged delivery model: "It's just 30 minutes, 2X per week, designed for high performers like you."

"I Need to Think About It"
Audit their baggage, own their losses, and bake that into your projected ROI. Reorient them to the dream, sell the second island (hello, coconuts, and WiFi), and keep them focused on *possibility*, not *affordability*. Because, at the end of the day, staying the same is more expensive than investing in change.

CHAPTER 10

Fulfillment Magic - Wow Your Clients and Keep Them Hooked

"The real voyage of discovery consists not in seeking new landscapes but in having new eyes."

– Marcel Proust

Honor your commitments. If you're even *thinking* about rescheduling a call because you're "just not feeling it," grab a copy of Steven Pressfield's *Turning Pro* and read it until the flakiness seeps out of your system. This industry can be flakier than a croissant in a windstorm, so show up on time, follow through, and own your slip-ups. You'll stand out like a unicorn in a parking lot.

Next up, protect your energy like it's your ATM password. Block toxic people and trolls as needed. The world's negativity supply is never-ending; you don't need that baggage in your next client session. But here's the twist: sometimes, a little "strategic forgiveness" works wonders.

Keeping bridges intact isn't just karma—it's career oxygen. Your network is like Wall Street: play it right, and it compounds faster than Belfort's penny stocks. Burn too many bridges, though, and you'll ghost yourself out of the game faster than Bud Fox post-Gekko.

"Keep your friends close and your haters closer"—they're basically unpaid interns for your PR. And as Robert Greene would say, "Never outshine the master." Unless, of course, you're Gordon Gekko's secret love child or plan to out-Belfort everyone with a yacht, a mic, and a questionable supply of Quaaludes.

On calls, try "listening between the lines." That means paying attention to what clients say and what they don't say. Think of it as psychic karaoke: you're mentally belting out their backstory while hearing their words. Some call it "deep listening" or "listening for insight." I like to imagine living in their shoes for a minute and tackling their problems like it's my reality show.

Developing this level of active listening is a superpower. It's like getting X-ray vision for client conversations. Be curious, care deeply, and radiate love (without getting too woo-woo on them). Encourage them to dive into your materials, role-play, and stay in touch between sessions. You're on-call 24/7, like a personal trainer for their brain.

Think about what they're *not* getting from other coaching programs—and make it so obvious they'll start wondering why they just blew $18K to sit on a Zoom call with 200 strangers and a guru rocking a gold watch, looking like a reformed frat bro who found Jesus... and a ClickFunnels subscription. Oh, and that sinking feeling? Yeah, it's because *you* are the product.

- **Personal attention.** Clients are over being just another square in a Brady Bunch grid. Give them tailored advice that *actually* solves their problems. Strategy? Locked. Tactics? Loaded. I'm basically the Cyrano de Bergerac of DMs—ghostwriting their lines, being their ultimate wingman, and making them look like a total mastermind while they kick back and take the credit.

- **Real-time, hands-on help.** Nobody offers this because they guard their calendars like Fort Knox. Fifteen-minute calls, ironclad schedules, and then—poof—they vanish like high-priced escorts after payday. You? Offer unlimited chat support (just add "within reason," unless 3 a.m. texts about their existential crises or "I had the weirdest dream about you!" is your thing).

- **Customized delivery.** Clients want to feel like you're adapting to *them*, not tossing them into some cookie-cutter program. Use frameworks like my *3 Walls* model or build a boot camp with small groups and specific pillars. Be nimble—it's your superpower. When a corporate manager says, "We need to role-play SPIN," or "Can we tackle rebuttals next time?" you flex and deliver. Ad hoc is the name of the game.

Troubleshooting: Energy Vampires

If a client is draining you dry, it's either a bad fit—or you're spending too much time starring in your own mental movie. On coaching calls, silence everything, including your ego. Be fully present. Make your client the headliner at Madison Square Garden and give them the full spotlight treatment.

Here's the cheat code: when you show up with 100% focus, curiosity, and *actual* attention, you can't lose. True "other orientation" is your ace card. Play it, and you'll create a polarity shift and close emotionally like a baller. And if you don't? At least you won't be another Zoom guru with bad lighting and 200 muted faces wondering what their $18K bought besides your ring light.

Time to Value—Secrets of Pricing, Packaging & Tiers

The moment a client hands over the cash, it's game on. The shot clock is ticking, and your job is to deliver value so fast they wonder if you've got magic powers. If you've nailed the seven steps, they've already had a mini "a-ha!" moment on the call. By investing in you, they signal, "I'm ready to transform!" (or at least stop procrastinating).

Don't let the momentum fizzle—hit them with homework right away! Assign a book like *Deep Work* by Cal Newport, *The 80/20 Principle* by Richard Koch, or *Atomic Habits* by James Clear. Bonus points if you send them a hefty chapter from your own book—because nothing says "get to work" like a deep dive into *your* wisdom. Early engagement not only speeds up their progress but also reassures them that they didn't just buy another online course—they bought *you*, the coach who isn't messing around.

I tend to run a quick goal exercise that dovetails into my sales superpowers-themed books:

1. 2025/2027/2030 goals
2. The goal behind each goal (what's driving you) - your why?
3. What's your superpower?
4. What's your greatest fear?

I ask them to prep this for me by the first call, and it's great to dig in deeper and get to know them better.

People ask me how to structure coaching, and I explain it as a logistics container for 1:1 and Group.

1:1 Coaching Structure

- We meet 2X weekly (30 min each)
- First, assess where you're at, your goals and challenges
- Customize the program
- Asynchronous chat and text (unlimited, within reason, lol)
- We collaborate on playbooks, docs, templates, scripts, etc.
- I take your chair and teach you everything I know to grow your pipeline 2-5X

Mastermind/Bootcamp Structure (Course - Certification)

- Workshops: We meet 1X weekly (1hr each)
- Secondary executive call 1X per week (30 min)
- Audit: First, assess where you're at, your goals, challenges, and seller bell curve (+OMG assessment)
- Customize the program
- Shared Team Slack: Asynchronous chat and unlimited text (within reason, lol)
- We collaborate on playbooks, docs, templates, scripts, etc.

Gamification possibilities

- Split into teams to foster competition.
- Quiz at the end of modules-pillars (If you do a 4-hour on-site workshop, break it into four pillars to reflect each hour. Break each hour down into half theory / half practice.)
- Managers judging role plays.
- Managers rate the best presentation with a prize.

Remember the "forgetting curve" that governs static webinars and teaching, 90%, is nearly immediately forgotten. Conversely, as you can see in the Learning Pyramid, "practicing doing a skill" or "teaching it to others" gives you 75-90% retention. (National Training Laboratories Institute)

When people ask what my program looks like, I tell them it's *custom*. "First, we shatter your income ceiling by identifying and breaking through limiting beliefs. Next, we uncover and leverage your unique zone of genius. Finally, I hand you the shortcuts I've learned from 24 years of experience, cutting through the noise so you can get results faster."

101, 202, 303 - Training Model

101 - Theoretical - learning the method

202 - Practical - role plays, drills in a safe space (competency transfer)

303 - Applying what you learned in the real world - field application (accountability)

Repeat after me to every client: "I'm a cash register, not a cost center."

Don't overdo it with your clients—it's like a weird paradox. They need time to actually go live their lives, work, and test your genius strategies. If you're a real expert coach, let them loose in the wild and stay in touch as they crush it. Therapists and mindset coaches? Sure, you can go deep for hours with longer sessions—different strokes for different folks.

So, pick your poison when it comes to scalable delivery: keep it streamlined, or risk becoming their 24/7 emotional support hotline, stress ball, or—worst of all—their personal emotional support peacock, fluffing your feathers to keep them entertained.

Trust me, too many coaches fall into this trap, and it's as tragic as it is hilarious.

Delivery Model Grab Bag

Team Workshops: Just 90 minutes a week for 1-3 months (plus a 30-minute exec call) and async Slack support. Believe it or not, that's all you need to confidently charge $10-25K a month—and have buttoned up corporate stiffs thanking you for it.

L&D: Leverage each rep's individual Learning & Development budget with manager approval—create a certification program (it qualifies as a course), and they can reimburse after you invoice. Plus, they get a snazzy badge on their LinkedIn profile. For larger teams, you can discount $1,500 per head down to $900, which turns into a quick $22K for running a 25-person, 1-month boot camp with four solid content pillars. Ian Koniak has this down to a science, regularly tapping into $5K annual stipends for his account executive programs.

Train the trainer: Offer a better deal if you train the main VP or the management layer. Over six weeks, I earned $30,000 training just the management team of a reputable Canadian investor relations platform, and they cascaded it down to the reps who were immediately effective in creating pipeline with it.

Transformative Coaching–Creating Lasting Change

Many people are stuck in victim mode, and as coaches, it's our job to help them realize, "Hey, you're the one holding the remote here." Or, as Steve Chandler says, "You've created a perfect system for the results you're getting." The ego loves its cozy corner, even if that means staying in a rut, making the same money, and replaying life's greatest hits of setbacks.

Call it karma on repeat or life stuck in airplane mode—like an elite personal trainer who refuses to let you skip leg day, a great coach doesn't just nudge but sometimes shoves you out of your comfort zone. That's exactly why clients are willing to pay top dollar: to have someone push them beyond what they believe possible.

In *Justin Michael Method 3.0: Attraction Selling*, I revealed everything I know about Manifestation and the Law of Attraction for sales—except one game-changing insight inspired by the brilliant Regan Hillyer. Drawing from Michael A. Singer's *The Surrender Experiment*, I discovered two powerful flavors of manifestation: the well-known "go-get-'em" approach and the lesser-known yet profoundly transformative "surrendered" method.

To master client acquisition, embrace both.

Manufactured Manifestation is the classic goal-setting approach: you jot down those 20MM goals, channel your inner Esther Hicks, and let the universe worry about the *how*.

Surrendered Manifestation is next level: stop paddling like a lunatic and let the river do the work. Why kill yourself going upstream when the universe already has a VIP cruise downstream? Michael Singer meditated in a field and accidentally floated into a tech empire. That's the art of letting go. And by the way, there are no accidents.

How do I apply this? I trust the right clients will show up exactly when I'm ready for them. Every morning, I wake up excited about who I might meet, unlike the panic-stricken coaches convinced "no one's buying." Surrender to a higher power, vibe with abundance, and rewire your mind to *expect* awesome clients who pay your full fees with a smile. That will become your 'new normal' reality.

And remember: clients don't sign up to be wowed by a "superhero coach" in a Teflon suit. If anything, they're afraid you'll see what a mess they are and that they'll flake on you like every other self-improvement plan. Just be real. Be humble. No flashy watches like Cardone or Miner—be the coach who's more "let's get real" than "let's flex for Instagram."

Take the Godfather of coaching, Steve Chandler. He strolls into a Fortune 500 for a coaching gig, and the sales leader asks, "What makes you qualified to coach my team?" Without missing a beat, Steve says, "I went bankrupt, my wife was committed, I survived AA, and my four kids think food is a daily requirement." The sales leader grins and says, "You're hired." Because clearly, nothing says *role model* like a personal highlight reel of disaster recovery.

Clients don't hold back because they doubt your skills—they hold back because they're terrified this might actually be the moment they have to face their own potential. Help them see that this time, they're *not* going to flake. This time, they won't give up. They're ready for a change, and they can trust you to walk with them through it. That trust isn't just why they'll sign up—it's why they'll stay, transform, and succeed.

Like *The Dummy Curve* in Sandler, you need to be "more *not* OK" than they are. *Be vulnerable*, share stories of your failures, and talk about how coaching transformed you. The more they open up, the more you can change them.

From the intake to the first call, your mission is clear:

- Dive so deep they'll think you're their emotional scuba instructor. Hold *the most powerful conversation of their life*.

- Uncover their secret dream—whether it's tearing through Monaco in an F1 car, running for president to outlaw pineapple pizza, ditching their 9-to-5 to become a DJ, or dating a supermodel and leaving DiCaprio sobbing into his Oscar, muttering, "How did I lose her?"
- Get them to spill what's really holding them back. Think part coach, part therapist, part detective uncovering the plot twist in a true crime docuseries faster than you can say, Benedict Cumberbatch.

Unlocking the Hot Mess:

1. What's their greatest fear? (Hint: It's not spiders; it's failure. #1 Answer? "Not living up to their potential.")

2. What's their secret dream? (It's more than "make money"; find the juicy details.)

3. How do they sabotage themselves? (Tequila as therapy, doom-scrolling humanity's downfall, buying a treadmill they'll never use, all while roasting themselves like it's a sport?)

4. Where have they thrown in the towel? (Check their graveyard of unfinished projects.)

5. What lies do they tell themselves about money? ("I'll save once I get a raise." Sure, you will!)

6. What's their biggest limiting belief? ("People like me don't succeed.")

7. What's their income ceiling? (What number makes them uncomfortable?)

8. Where's their comfort zone? (Spoiler: nothing good happens there.)

9. How are they afraid of letting *you* down? ("What if I'm the one person coaching can't fix?")
10. What fixed ideas do they have about themselves? ("I'm not a leader," or "I'm bad with money.")
11. Can they shift from victim to owner? ("Mercury retrograde isn't ruining your life, Karen.")

Without this level of intimacy, they'll stay stuck and never take the plunge to invest. My first calls are like diffusing a land mine: skepticism, baggage, and doubts ticking away while I cut through the BS to help them see the dream.

As Jay Abraham says: "If you're the most *interested* person in the world, you'll be the most *interesting* person in the world."

How to Coach Without Being a Jerk

- Serve clients so powerfully they'll name their firstborn after you (or at least consider it).
- Be vulnerable, humble, and brutally candid. Sugarcoating is for donuts.
- Share your flaws and failures like war stories; show how coaching saved your bacon.
- Make it OK that they're a hot mess. "You're a mess? Same. Let's get to work."
- Reduce friction by acknowledging and empathizing like you're customer service for their soul.
- Spot the gold in them they can't see, and hype it up like it's Mike Tyson vs. Jake Paul.
- Be fascinated by them. Curiosity is love, and *love wins*.

Master this level of raw, unfiltered connection, and you'll close the gap between doubt and commitment faster than they can say, "Take my money!"

Beyond The 3rd Wall: Referrals, Renewals, and LTV Curves

After 3 to 6 months, many clients think they've cracked the code and are ready to graduate. But here's the trick, straight from Bryan Franklin, who once coached Reid Hoffman: "The more mysterious you are, the higher you can charge." So if you want clients to stick around, you've got to keep that air of mystery, like the coaching world's David Blaine.

Keep them guessing! Vary your delivery algorithm. Stack model after model, layer upon layer—one month, you're the fundraising guru; the next, the team-building whisperer. Avoid "spilling all your candy in the lobby," as Sandler warned. Instead, dole out those insights like a Netflix cliffhanger—just when they think they know what's coming, hit them with a plot twist.

Familiarity breeds contempt, but variety is the spice of life—or maybe the spice of *Dune* to turn their eyes glowing blue with awe. Choose your spice wisely!

When I started, I blasted through content like a firehose, and, surprise, it was overwhelming. Effective coaching is more of a slow-burn art form. Take a tip from ex-teachers like Josh Braun and Chris Caldwell, who know how to pace their genius (probably from years of keeping 8th graders from setting things on fire). Working with teacher and math whiz clients inspired me to develop the "Monetization Diamond" approach—a game-changing method that breaks cold calls into manageable modules; each focused on mastering a specific micro-skill. This isn't just about quick wins; it's a proven foundation for lasting expertise and long-term success.

To keep clients hooked, your content library has to be deeper than Prince's song catalog. I'm talking seven books, 17 guides, and endless topics to zoom in or out. If you're a sales leader, you can always find another angle—train their trainers, overhaul their messaging, optimize their tech stack. You're a Swiss Army knife, not a single-use gadget.

And on referrals: forget blasting your email list with "Send me your friends!" Take it slow. Get on a 1:1 call, catch up, and walk them through the referral process like you're introducing them to the secret menu. Shotgun referrals don't work; everyone would do it if they did. Offer a referral fee they can apply to their coaching *with you*—make it tempting. And while some top coaches have armies of appointment-setters and closers, I keep it personal. When I take things slow and do everything myself, it's got that handcrafted feel, like a Swiss watch or a Savile Row suit.

Time to renew? Sweeten the deal to seal the commitment. If they initially signed up for a three-month plan but only paid for one, offer the previously upfront three-month discount as an incentive when they're ready to go all in. I steer clear of pay-as-you-go or split-payment deals—they often lead to early drop-offs and lack of accountability.

Pro Tip: Todd Caponi is the king of deal levers, and here's a game-changing insight: upfront payments are always better—thank you, time-value of money! Longer commitments (term) create stability, and the more reps clients get with you (just like a fitness routine), the greater the value they'll experience (scope). Craft a strategic list of "give-to-get" levers: "Sure, you can have that 30% discount, but in return, I'll need a glowing testimonial *once* you crush your goals." It's a win-win—delivering results while securing your worth.

And here's the kicker: sometimes, clients will start looking for reasons to bail just to dodge the bill. It's sneaky! They may not even know they're doing it. That's why it's best to get paid upfront. They'll dive in with both feet when they've got natural skin in the game. Once they're fully invested—emotionally and financially—they'll show up, give it their all, and truly change. It takes 21 days to rewire the brain, but a little upfront commitment will make the difference.

The House Painter Metaphor

John Patrick Morgan told this story about client attraction that sounds like it's straight out of a medieval legend. Picture a legendary blacksmith crafting such epic swords that knights would trek for miles to get their hands on one.

Now, flash forward: a house painter rolls into town, finds the shabbiest, most paint-peeling house on the block, and decides to go full makeover mode. The tenants are away, and when they get back, *bam!* Their place is gleaming in gloss white. The painter leaves a stack of business cards in the mailbox, and soon enough, neighbors are pulling up like, "Who made your house look like that?" Cue business cards flying out the door.

The idea? Find one person. Blow their mind with transformation. They'll be your walking billboard, spreading the word. And soon, just like Steve Martin said (and Cal Newport wrote a book about), you'll "be so good they can't ignore you."

News spreads fast when you're doubling incomes, revealing hidden purposes, or cranking up someone's self-esteem to 11. Jesus healed a few people, and suddenly, a line stretched to the horizon. The same thing happens with clients. If you focus on genuinely helping *one* person, a village will come beating down your door.

Pro Tip: In your next session, channel your inner Daniel Day-Lewis, go full *Method Acting* on their situation, become *them*, and crack their code through their eyes, like you're gunning for an Oscar.

The Top 10 Deadly Sins Coaches Fall For (Drumroll, Please!)

Alright, here it is, David Letterman fans—your Top 10 Coaching Blunders that will have you spinning your wheels like a pro! (Or, you know, at least keep you broke and baffled.)

#10: Giving free consulting

- Because who doesn't love working for free? Next up: unpaid therapy and pro bono life advice!

#9: Spending all your time on branding and marketing

- Ah yes, the classic "famous on Instagram, invisible in the bank account" strategy.

#8: Comparing yourself to other coaches

- Nothing screams "success" like constantly questioning your worth while scrolling through LinkedIn at 3 a.m.!

#7: Rushing (slow down, you're not a caffeinated squirrel)

- Slow and steady wins the race…unless you move so slowly, even a tortoise passes you.

#6: The Tender Trap - Pluralism!

- Who needs one happy client when you can half-serve a mob? Genius move. Rushing to shotgun clients just scares off the good ones. Want a winning cohort? Enroll 'em old school—one at a time.

#5: Trying too hard

- Face it: needy = creepy. No one likes a coach who's as clingy as a college ex.

#4: Ignoring your 1st circle warm leads

There is nothing like stepping over piles of cash to chase cold leads in Antarctica!

#3: Not asking for referrals

- Here's a pro tip: offer 20% off referrals. Money talks, and you can stop doing all the talking.

#2: Over-niching

- Why serve a broad audience when you can target that hyper-niche market of left-handed llama herders?

And the #1 Coaching Blunder…Building emotional walls with clients

- Nothing says "I care" like keeping clients at arm's length. "I'm here to help…but not too much."

Avoid these, and who knows—you might just make it as a coach without becoming a motivational meme.

CHAPTER 11

Automate, Win Corporates, Perfect Delivery

"You gotta BE before you can DO and DO before you can HAVE."

—Zig Ziglar

So many coaches come to me looking like Neo after dodging too many bullets, gripping their bank accounts like they've just realized the Matrix is real, and they're running out of time. They're on the "lumpy" revenue roller coaster—one moment channeling their inner John Wick, walking into a room like "Yeah, I got this," and the next, Googling, "How to get a W-2 job without looking desperate," as if the High Table is after them.

The fix? Lock and load your practice with 15-25 clients, even if it means temporarily lowering your fees. As Robert Greene cryptically states in *Mastery:* "You're here to master your craft so profoundly that the world has no choice but to pay attention." Translation? Jam-pack that pipeline like a trunk full of tactical gear, and suddenly, your income roller coaster feels less like a car chase through Rome and more like a slow cruise to Zion. (Or, as Jeb Blount might monotone like Morpheus: "The pipe is life.")

While you're building toward that dream Monthly Recurring Revenue (MRR)—your business's version of reloading mid-gunfight—you need to commit 80% of your time to prospecting. Yes, 80%. Think of it as your red pill moment: you can pretend the pipeline will magically fill itself, or you can face the reality that 3-5 "Are we a fit?" (Aaron Ross AWAF) calls per day is what keeps you in the fight. And even when your calendar is stacked higher than Wick's body count, you *still* need to prospect. Why? Because nothing empties faster than a pipeline you've stopped filling—think of it as Neo unplugging from the Matrix mid-fight. Not good.

"Perfect is the enemy of progress." — Voltaire (or maybe it was the Oracle after making cookies). Forget perfection. Run LinkedIn automation like it's your arsenal, send 100 invites weekly, blast 800 open-profile messages, and DM every first-degree connection like you're calling for backup at The Continental. Will it be messy? Absolutely. But messy, consistent action is your tactical advantage. Build that pipeline, master your craft, and soon your coaching business won't just survive—it'll thrive, like Neo leveling up or John Wick casually dismantling 40 enemies without breaking a sweat.

You can program your *Automation du jour* to:

- Send 40 1st degree personalized messages per day
- Add 100 targeted connections/week (LinkedIn caps at 400/mo—no need to speed like it's the Indy 500).
- Slowly add 800 Open Profiles 2nd degree (or risk LinkedIn slapping you like a bouncer at a VIP club).

Pro Tip: Do the targeting yourself in Sales Nav. Why? Because automation loves throwing curveballs—ask for CEOs, get Linda the massage therapist. Connection requests are gold—don't spend them like Monopoly money.

- Set up your first message, aka the "spark" (something better than your best Ryan Gosling "Hey girl").
- Handle the first back-and-forth yourself.
- Once connected, drop your opening like it's hot and watch the magic unfold.

Prospecting is just like prayer; cue Madonna. Prospect unceasingly.

I've survived every rollercoaster—recessions, pandemics, and those random "what am I doing with my life" slumps—by keeping my foot glued to the gas pedal, even on the downhills. Think of *Combo Prospecting*, *Tech-Powered Sales*, and *The JMM Trilogy* as your instruction manual for building momentum, no matter the bumps.

When you start a coaching business, the first few months are like the honeymoon phase. Clients from your inner circle flock to you, and life feels like a sales highlight reel. Then, bam! Six months in, you hit the *plateau of doom*. You're feeling tapped out, and suddenly, you're like, "Where did everyone go?" That's where I come in—to lead you up the "slope of enlightenment" (sounds Gartner-level fancy, right?) and get you back to a steady, sustainable flow.

Trust me, my clients hit slumps all the time. Remember: if you've done it once, you can do it again. There are tens of millions of prospects, and only one *you*. Clients are out there; it's time to dust off that confidence. Reread those glowing testimonials, grab some sleep, reset, and get back out there with fresh energy. Start having conversations about *anything*—Steve Chandler says, "Every sale happens *within* a conversation," and he's not wrong. So go chat someone up and let the magic begin.

Scaling Clients Without Overload

The secret to building a thriving coaching business? Surprisingly simple.

Think of it like cooking. You need a balanced "menu" of clients to keep things cooking just right. On the back burner, you have those slow-brewing corporate deals, like VPs, that need 45-120 days to simmer before they're ready. And don't even mention 30-day "net terms." I'm not your loan shark—I'm just here for the *actual* money, thanks! On the front burner? Fast-cooking 1:1 coaching clients, who you can "close and serve" in 1-2 calls if the timing's perfect. Group programs? They are excellent as a "gateway drug," but remember—the big bucks are in 1:1 customization.

Here's a hack: say "custom" and "bespoke" at every chance. This can boost your fees, close rate, and deal speed by 10X. It's like magic. People will pay $99 to be one of a thousand on a call with Arnold Schwarzenegger, but they'll fork over $10,000 to spend a day with him alone. Customization sells. Make it your mantra.

Jacco van der Kooij calls it "stackable revenue bricks." Translation: Keep it simple. Stack a few solid offers you can handle. I learned this the hard way. In month 6, I juggled 40 clients—hopping on calls, building scripts and white papers, handling RevOps, and fixing tech stacks. I was trying to be the Bo Jackson of coaching—dominating mindset baseball, strategy football, and emotional track and field—until I burned out so hard, it was like his bat snapped over *my* knee.

Even with a team, the workload was chaos. From 6 a.m. to 3 a.m., I was downing Red Bull like water and still losing clients. Worse, it felt like "turn to page 16 for your generic coaching plan" instead of the fun, creative 1:1 customization that makes coaching exciting.

So, write down every service you can monetize to scale without losing your sanity. Pick the top three ways you *like* to work. Bundle a few retainer packages, roll them out, and stack them. My sweet spot? Working with teams of up to 10 reps for $15K/month on a three-month minimum retainer. That's $45K, or $36K if they pay upfront. I've pared down my offerings to 1:1 coaching and team workshops since those are the easiest to stack.

KISS! Keep it stupidly simple and custom, and watch your clients and your energy stay with you.

Closing Corporate Clients—Your Cash Cow

What's the secret sauce behind the world's top companies? Believe it or not, up to 40% use executive coaching to stay ahead of the pack (Hay Group International). And here's the wild part—a Metrix Global study says coaching delivers a mind-blowing 788% ROI, boosting productivity, retaining top talent, and fattening the bottom line.

I'll never forget an intake call Josh Braun led with a VP and their team. He opened with: "Who here has a growth mindset and actually *wants* this training?" Silence. Then, the split: growth mindset folks vs. the "I'd rather wing it" crowd. Too often, companies toss reps to the "training lions" with zero buy-in and then wonder why morale is tanking. For coaching to work, you need people who *want* to be there. Savvy managers know this and pick growth-hungry, motivated reps who are just itching for that next level. That's where fundamental transformation happens.

The Bell Curve is catnip! When I chat ROI with CROs, I say, "Let's move your middle performers up and to the right." Then I ask, "Tell me about your team—who's on the way out, who's stuck in the middle, and who are your rockstars?" This sets the ROI stage and shows them that this training will differ. Suddenly, they're paying attention.

Corporate clients are the slow cookers of the business world—some take 90 days, and others take 3 years to close. Chet Holmes says 3% are ready to buy anytime, but 40% could be persuaded. It's a numbers game, but you've got to play it smart.

My book of business has two flavors of clients: action-takers I coach directly and managers of action-takers. Talkers be damned! One of my best moves has been sneaking into companies through a front-line champion, like an SDR or team manager, who's used my Codices to crush their targets. It's like dropping a tiny seed in the soil and watching it grow into a big money tree.

The biggest mistake I see consultants make is going straight for the CEOs and founders, hoping to make a single heroic pitch. They shoot too high and get ghosted. Sometimes, the imaginative play is to team up with one person or division, help them crush it, and let the results bubble up the ladder.

Case in point: I closed a $300K deal because an SDR leader got my guides off Reddit *three years ago*. He used them to rack up 80 net new F1000 opportunities with a Venn diagram, of all things. Leadership changed, a bid opened with three new trainers, and I won because I'd already proven my chops. That's what happens when you start at the ground level—you end up *owning* the whole building.

Here's an example of Aaron Norris generating a meeting with a corporate team enablement leader.

"A referral post tag turned into a multi-threaded outreach win. I WhatsApped the referrer, ghost-wrote a reply for them, and then connected directly with the sales leader and enablement lead. I dove right into their goals in DMs, secured an intro to enablement from the sales leader, and even sweetened the deal with a referral incentive to keep the original referrer engaged. Quick action, targeted engagement, and strategic incentives—transforming a tag into tangible leads!"

Corporations are just groups of *individuals*, so the 7-step process works just as effectively—the only difference is longer sales cycles due to all the red tape. It's bureaucracy-central! My focus is on team leads with 5-15 years of experience, typically from director level to CRO. I engage them with open-ended questions about their team's performance, goals, and challenges, ensuring the conversation is both relevant and insightful.

Delivery? I only hold weekly workshops and then have an executive call weekly or bi-weekly, with unlimited access to shared Slack and asynchronous doc collaboration. On that call, we discuss the progress of individual team members. And that's it! I learned this model from greats like Aaron Ross. You can't constantly be with the client and their team because then they're *not* selling during the golden hours.

You will often get baked off against other trainers, so the secret to winning a training RFP like the one I just closed for $300,000 to train 600 sellers is to have a hardcore champion evangelize for you from the inside.

I shipped my books to all the five decision-makers in this deal. I tailored my pitch on each call. I worked with my champion on the pitch deck and presentation, even the GANTT chart of how the rollout would happen globally. He spoke the internal love language, and I beat out another rival trainer who charged less and had even worked with this SVP before. One bidder was such a JMM™ clone, it felt like a scene out of *Multiplicity*—but not Michael Keaton #1, more like clone #4. The SVP's eyebrow said it all!

Why did I win? My open-source, flexible framework could be wrapped around their existing McKinsey plays and tech stack, like Sales Nav, ZoomInfo, Outreach, etc. My focus on tech-enabled systems, frameworks, and formulas brought the RevOps team to the table, the glue between Sales and Marketing in an ABM approach.

Delivery Models (Team Training)

You'll either get some funds cleared with Enablement or from the Marketing budget to get a fee for a boot camp (30 days) or retainer work (90 days), or you'll need to plug into individual L&D budgets. Most provide about $1.5K per rep (per year), which is not enough for your 1:1 premium executive coaching, but it can contribute. Remember, if you coach sales development reps (SDRs), 40% of them roll up to Marketing (per Bridge Group).

30-Day Bootcamp Course

Four pillars of prospecting or closing
Role-play, exercise, and theory.
Customizable
Certification provided (badge on profile)
L&D budget $1,500 per rep (sliding scale over 10 reps)

You'll be handling a lot of invoicing since each participant gets reimbursed individually, but a boot camp with ten reps can quickly rack up over $15K in revenue. The best part? It's faster cash—participants can charge it to their credit cards right away instead of waiting for procurement's net-30 process.

1-off Workshop

- 3 hours
- Six subjects
- Three roleplays

Commercials:
$10-25K
Everything is customized, especially the decks and role-plays beforehand.

My preferred structure for corporate training?

Group Coaching

- 3-months - Standard retainer
- Weekly workshops (60-90 min)
- Weekly executive calls (30 min)
- Role-plays, drills on the workshops – possible quizzes
- Async access in shared Team Slack (share wins, call recordings, replies, etc.)
- Audit calls, create playbooks (for future new hires), collab on scripts, tear down emails

Commercials:
$15,000/mo / minimum 3 months
($45K rack rate / $36K if paid upfront)

Build Your Own Full-Cycle Menu: Design a personalized roadmap for your sales process, structured like a funnel. Start with prospecting, flow through progression, and finish with closing. For each stage, outline the key skills you teach, along with the steps, tools, and strategies that support your workflow. Looking for ideas? DM me, and I'll share an example of my most effective setup!

Additional Tips for Closing Corporates: (Aka, Herding Cats in Suits)

- **Work with your champion.** They're your ride-or-die for getting the deal through. Coach them 1:1 to showcase your brilliance, then let them parade your magic up the command chain like you're a corporate unicorn.

- **New decision-maker? New cycle.** When a new senior exec shows up, don't just dust off the same pitch. Hit the reset button and start wooing them like it's date night all over again.

- **Don't get spooked by big fees.** Instead of wondering, "Am I really worth $10K a month?" flip the script: "What's their ROI?" If they close one $50K deal and you cost $30K for three months, you're already ROI-positive. Plus, the downstream pipeline could add millions. Congrats, you just became a bargain.

- **The audit trick.** Want to break into a corporate engagement? Offer a $5K-$15K audit to "peek under the hood." Trust me, what's under there won't be a finely tuned engine—it'll look like a clown car that crashed into a fireworks factory: parts flying, smoke everywhere, and the horn stuck on a desperate wheeze. The best part? You'll uncover $90K+ in chaos practically begging to be fixed. Cha-ching.

Take this report from a client's recent audit:

- No idea how to generate pipeline with cold outbound.
- Quota targets that shift more than a politician's promises.

- SalesLoft sequences so canned they belong in a pantry.
- Training that's all *"Here's our product,"* and zero *"Here's how it helps."*
- Business value? Nope, straight to pricing.
- A VP of Sales who openly admits the quotas are unattainable and feels *bad* holding reps to them.

That's not a company; that's a jigsaw puzzle missing half the pieces, advertising itself as a masterclass in efficiency. As my dad used to say when I whined about startups: "Startups are Warren Buffett's cigar with one puff left. Be grateful for the opportunity! If they weren't a beautiful disaster, why would they need *your* help?" Their mess is your opportunity.

Certifications: To ICF or Not to ICF?

Sure, certifications like the International Coaching Federation (ICF) or Co-Active Coaching can get you on the "approved internal coach" list for some corporates, and they can help you systematize your delivery. But the highest-earning coaches I know? They don't have fancy credentials. What they *do* have is thousands of hours coaching real people. So get the certification if it makes sense—but don't let it be your crutch. Your results will always speak louder than your résumé.

Troubleshooting: Be the NFL's Cryo-Coach, Not the Play Caller

Think of yourself as the NFL's "strength and conditioning coach," not the head coach barking plays on the field. Why? Because VPs get territorial—sometimes hilariously hostile—when they think you're a third-party trainer swooping in to show them up. So disarm them with humor:

"Don't worry, John, you're the lead coach. I'm just here to take the team into the cryo-chamber, dunk them in the ice bath like Wim Hof, and teach them upside-down handstand pushups and backflips."

This instantly neutralizes their competitiveness and reframes you as the secret weapon, not the threat. Add this gem:

"Bringing me in shows your team you're investing in their success. Most companies wouldn't even consider hiring an external coach—it's rare, and it's powerful."

It's true. Across the 13 companies I've worked for, only two ever invested in formalized training (Challenger and Sandler). The rest? Like a reality TV show—high drama, no strategy. Just wing it, hope for the best and let the CRO "super close" deals with a mix of charm and sheer panic.

Pro Tip: How to Nail Your SKO and Day Rates

Oren Klaff taught me to price Sales Kickoffs (SKOs) at $25K, with travel and hotel included. Virtual? Drop it to $15K—because, hey, you're not raiding the minibar. For perspective, an infamous UK trainer charges $7K/day, Chris Caldwell makes $15K/day, and Tony J. Hughes charges $5K/month for two "human days" (whatever *that* means). Still way cheaper than hiring an FTE who needs a 401(k) and "unlimited" PTO.

Fun fact: hiring anyone in a Tier 1 city costs $100K+, even if they think "BANT" is a kind of sandwich. Meanwhile, Caldwell raked in $144K in a week, thanks to SKOs. Famous Training Co.? They charge $25K just to show up and say, "Believe in yourself!" So, own your rate—it's a steal compared to hiring someone who needs Slack tutorials and vape breaks to survive.

The Best Rate Rebuttal Ever

If they try to haggle, drop this mic-worthy line:

"If I lower my rate, what does that teach your sales team when *your* prospects ask for discounts?"

CEO: "You're right. We'll pay the full fee upfront."

Boom. No discounts, no drama—just the respect (and rate) you deserve.

CHAPTER 12

Scaling to 100K/Month - Content, Delegation, and Cohort Mixology

"The more people on the call, the less you pay."

– Jamal Reimer

Stacking revenue isn't about living in "implementation purgatory," where your life becomes an endless loop of spreadsheets and Zoom calls. The real magic happens in the high-impact zone—where your brilliance shines, not grinds. Stick to implementation, and you're juggling 2-4 clients, max. Switch to strategy—getting paid to *think*, not do—and suddenly scaling to 15+ clients is as easy as Friday night takeout. As David C. Baker wisely says in *The Business of Expertise*, strategy and implementation are two rooms connected by a hallway—shut the implementation door, and you stop being just another commodity. The payoff? You scale like someone who charges for blueprints, not just bricks.

The goal? Don't be the "doer" buried in the trenches. Be the "sage on the mountain"—the one people go to for big-picture magic. The less you roll up your sleeves, the more you're stacking revenue and scaling like a boss.

Picture this: you're hopping on calls for $7K monthly with three clients—$21K total. That's nice, but you're maxed out if you're doing all the gritty work yourself. Instead, "shut the execution door." Take one or two hands-on clients and then stack up on pure advisory. Imagine it: no more heavy lifting, just high-level 1:1 strategy sessions, GTM coaching, and sales role-plays. Hit $100K months solo? It's not wild if you layer up like this. Call it your personal revenue "layer cake"—delicious and profitable, without getting crumbs on your hands.

Anatomy of a $100,000 Month:
$60,000 in 1:1s
5 * 1:1 clients at 5K * 3mos, paid upfront w/ a 20% discount
(5 X 12K = 60K)

+ $36,000 in Team Workshops
1 team $15,000/mo for three months w/ a 20% discount if paid upfront. Workshops on a proven outbound method.
($45,000 X 20%) $36,000

+ $5,000 in Intensives
1 $5K 2-hour intensive, or making a cameo on a team call to give a mini-workshop. My record was earning $7,000 for 20 minutes of tactics for a CRM company once.

I always start with a three-month minimum because, let's face it, in the first 30-45 days, clients hit the *Trough of Disillusionment* harder than a toddler coming down from a sugar high (hat tip Gartner Hype Cycle). That's the danger zone where they're wondering why they signed up. Stick with me, though, because after that? Boom—*Slope of Enlightenment*. A

Venn Diagram

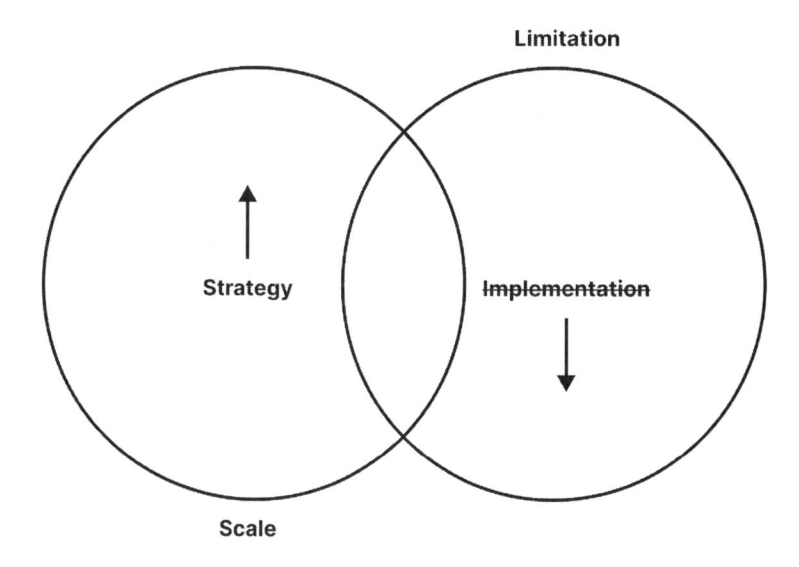

- **Limitation**: Implementation (↓)
- **Scale**: Strategy (↑)

one-month stint? That's just begging for a 4/10 Yelp review, and nobody wants that. Ninety days is where the magic happens.

Get creative with pricing. Start with a $500-$1K/week package—ideal for clients who want success without maxing out their credit cards. Or go big with a $25K-50K sorcerer's apprenticeship, where you go full-on Gandalf mode, mentoring them for 6-12 months like you're their personal wizard-in-residence. At least you're not charging $1MM to shout "UNLEASH YOUR POWER" while they fry their feet on hot coals à la Tony Robbins.

Feeling fancy? Offer a Bali retreat because, apparently, breakthroughs only happen after $20 smoothies and a group cry by a waterfall. Not into Bali? Host it somewhere "elevated" (read: within Uber range) where the fanciest thing is solid Wi-Fi. Prefer something steady? Try six months of bi-weekly calls—or crank it up with 30-minute HIIT-style coaching that's like CrossFit for their brain. I toss them strategies and say, "Crush it—and if anyone brings up firewalking, just smile and back away slowly."

You can thrive on volume, too. I've done 275+ invoices in a year, leaving other coaches gobsmacked. But some, like Bryan Franklin, take the "forever" model: $25K up front, then $5K/month on autopilot, keeping clients for 2-5 years. It's all about knowing your Serengeti style—are you a cheetah, lion, or gazelle? Either way, anchor your fees high from the start and act like you belong there.

Long-term positioning is key. Don't offer a month, cross your fingers and hope they'll upgrade. Instead, pitch 12 months, 6 months, or 3 months right out of the gate, with discounts for paying upfront. Example: $50K for 12 months, $25K for 6 months, $12K for 3 months. Knock off 20% if they pay upfront. Oh, and one more thing: no refunds.

If you see greatness in someone, offer monthly payments—but only if they've got skin in the game. Without mutual commitment, they'll treat your coaching like an ayahuasca retreat—lots of deep talks and puking, but no real-life follow-through. Transformation needs stakes, not just visions of a new you! (By the way, Lizard people are real; I've reported to them.)

Finally, avoid hourly rates like they're radioactive. Charging hourly makes it harder for clients to justify the investment, and it cheapens your value. As Alan Weiss says, "It's unethical to charge by the hour because it incentivizes me to drag things out instead of delivering results." Translation? High-impact outcomes deserve high-impact fees. So, ditch the clock, embrace the value, and charge like you mean it.

If you want to scale your coaching, consulting, or advisory business, start by solving one universal problem for a niche or vertical. Then, flip it horizontally like a pancake at a brunch buffet. I guide my clients through this, but let's be real—I solve the top funnel for *ANYONE*. I'm like a rare Pokémon now—scarce but with legions of prospects chasing me. Abundance unlocked.

DE-NICHING

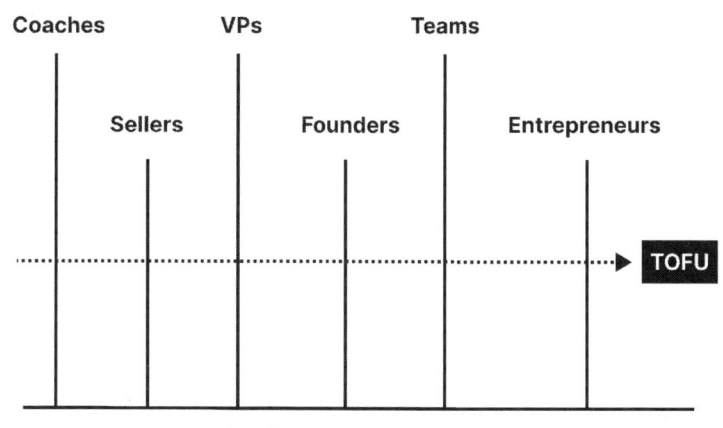

```
Coaches        VPs          Teams
   |            |             |
   |   Sellers  |   Founders  |   Entrepreneurs
   |     |      |     |       |     |
   |     |      |     |       |     |
   ·······································▶ [TOFU]
   |     |      |     |       |     |
```

Moving from vertical to horizontal

TOFU = top of funnel

Want to level up? Grab *Million Dollar Consulting Proposals* by the almighty Alan Weiss and start playing with these ideas. Always build customized proposals collaboratively, like a shared Google Doc masterpiece. Begin with simple headers to lock down the conversation, such as:

North Star Goals:

- Deliverables
- Logistics
- Curriculum
- Commercials:

    (Don't forget to include a deeper discount for a 6-month renewal here / speak to the go-forward plan upon successful completion of the 90 days and ROI)

- Case studies

    (Ping me for a boilerplate copy of a *JMM*-style collaborative proposal template)

Talking money over email is like trying to sell a parachute to someone over the phone while they're skydiving—no context, no connection, and they'll probably disappear on you mid-sentence.

Pro-tip on nailing Commercials: Alan Weiss and my experience in charity fundraising working for Sean Parker at Causes.com confirm *The Choice of Multiple Yeses*. Always include three levels of pricing because 80% of the time, they pick the middle option.

'Choice of Yeses' - Alan Weiss-inspired Example:

Option 1:
1:1 coaching for your VP for 90 days = $15K (5K/mo * 3 months) or 20% off upfront ($12K)

Option 2:
Team coaching for 90 days - $45K up to 10 reps (15K/mo * 3 months) or 20% off paid upfront ($36K)

Option 3:
Six months paid upfront = 30% off either Option 1 or 2

Get creative with pricing, but always include a "why-does-this-even-exist" low option and a high fee so outlandish it sounds like you're trying to fund a moon mission. Most clients will gravitate towards the middle, feeling like financial geniuses for picking the "Goldilocks" plan.

Now, when they try to negotiate, stay cool. If they ask, "Can you cut me a deal?" hit them with, "Well, John, considering the ROI on just two of your deals is $100K, you're practically robbing me at this price." And when Karen asks for a shorter term, fire back with, "Look, Karen, it takes 21 days to form a habit. Neuroplasticity, baby. Let's go 90 days so you don't relapse into bad LinkedIn posts." Clients will push back, but as Mike Bosworth says, they're just "squeezing the towel"—so anchor high, stand firm, and keep reminding them why they're here: to make money, not friends.

To keep them laser-focused, tag them in a shared "proposal sketch" doc under "North Star Goals" and make them edit it. If they add something absurd, like "5X pipeline in 90 days," tone it down to "Work *toward* 5Xing pipeline in 90 days." Under-promise and over-deliver—that way, when you triple their pipeline instead of quintupling it, they'll still feel like they hit the jackpot. Clear expectations prevent churn, and if you throw in the occasional surprise 1:1, they'll think you're a hero, not just doing your job.

Oh, and boundaries are everything. Once I capped 1:1 calls to two 30-minute slots a week and shifted teams to workshops only, my hourly rate shot through the roof. Now, I handle 25+ clients at a time, impacting hundreds of reps with workshops while keeping my private clients limited to a select few getting premium "love and support"—DMs, docs, the works. I'm like the sales coach version of John Wick—calm, precise, and unstoppable. I don't "implement"; I execute.

That's why you've got to pick a consulting niche that feels as natural as breathing. When you align your gifts with your talents, you'll stay in flow, cranking out brilliance without pulling all-nighters or staring blankly at a screen. It's like Bruce Lee's philosophy—be like water: adaptable, powerful, and always finding its way to flow effortlessly around obstacles.

So, do what you love, and you'll never work another day in your life—or at least, you'll look like you're having fun doing it. After all, Zig Ziglar said it best: "You can have everything you want in life if you'll just help enough other people get what they want."

And remember, as Dale Carnegie put it: "You can make more friends in two months by pretending to care about people than in two years of them pretending to care about you." Wait, is that how he said it? Close enough.

Books & Content–Creating Ultra-High Intent Leads

Adapted from Naval Ravikant, this strategy with a little Alex Hormozi *beard over muscle-shirt* flavor maps out the holy grail of scaling leverage. At the start, before you've got capital to throw around, the best leverage is content. Become a content machine. Crank out posts, videos, blogs, and bam—you will influence status (and cash flow). With that cash, you can invest in scalable assets like code. Eventually, you'll have the resources to build a team and become the business equivalent of a one-person band with a full orchestra backing you up like Michael Bublé.

The secret weapon? Recycling and repurposing your content.

Save everything when you deliver a workshop, training, or coaching session. You're building an arsenal of decks, videos, podcasts, and guides—a master key to unlock new possibilities and a versatile toolkit you can customize to tackle each client's unique challenges. Five years in, I've got a treasure trove of assets—interviews, templates, guides—you name it. Content leverage is like the sourdough starter of your business: keep feeding it, and it'll keep delivering value for your clients *and* your bottom line.

Looking back over the past five years, I've nailed my formula: start with books—super-high intent magnets. Add hundreds of YouTube interviews. That combo brought in capital, which I funneled into building teams, code, and projects like a startup version of Sherwood Forest. Alan Weiss says, "One book is an anomaly, but three books make you an expert."

So I kept writing, dropping content breadcrumbs—Lars Nilsson-style ABSD spreadsheets and Codex cheat codes—so people could track me down like I was hiding out in the woods. Reddit banned me for "selling," but I was just playing Robin Hood: giving new reps techniques that generate billions in pipeline while the old trainers are still bragging about cold calls they made on landlines during the Reagan administration.

The trick to cranking out content? Parkinson's Law—work expands to fit the time available. Goals are dreams with deadlines. Want to finish a book? Set a target of 30-45K words by the end of the quarter. Get up, take your coffee, and write for an hour or two every morning. Start with an outline, then pour it all onto the page like you're just talking to your clients. Writing a book doesn't have to take years; set a date and sprint. Done.

Do the same with YouTube. Through your content, lead fans on a "treasure hunt." I once found a hidden gem about "chat flows" in an episode with Ankush Jain and emailed him immediately to send me a guide. People love a good Easter egg.

Want more? Start a Substack or Medium blog, firing off spontaneous hot takes whenever inspiration hits. Prospects will follow your updates like a hawk (and maybe even pay a few bucks for the privilege). I've even broken the news inside private groups, dropping info like a mic, only to watch it spread like wildfire. The best leak? The one you've engineered.

If you open-source your I.P., make sure credit comes with it. My work's been "borrowed" so much my fans police it like Banksy's street art. With *JMM*™ staples like Venn Diagrams, "thoughts?" bumps, and RRM call openers, my style is so distinct that copycats get exposed faster than a *Bachelor* secret after two glasses of wine. So, will your legacy be Milli Vanilli or Eddie Van Halen? Choose wisely.

Power of Delegation—Leveraging Subcontractors

I've got a squadron of virtual assistants (VAs) covering everything from data wrangling and social media antics to YouTube stardom, B2B wizardry, and animation magic. One of my favorite power moves? Deploying VAs to run my *4th frame* strategy—like that crew I had in Denmark, logging into my LinkedIn profile to kickstart conversations and tee up $15K in billings. Trust me, it's like having a secret army.

Top coaches, like Ian Koniak, have leveled up by hiring a Head of Business Development to handle outreach and prospecting—cloning yourself without cloning the Chevy Chase dad jokes. I've mentored many Gen Zs under my business umbrella and even have a 20% referral offer that attracts the bold and brilliant.

There's the "hands-on artisan" approach—doing it all yourself, like Bond trying to defuse a bomb while holding a martini and charming a Bond girl. Or you could hand off bookings, chat rooms, and Kajabi to a community manager—that's like having your own Q, whipping up gadgets while you sip your martini, and taking all the credit for saving the day.

Need leads? I know VAs who could find the Yeti and Jimmy Hoffa if you asked them to. They human-verify cell numbers, write email sequences, and warm up 15+ email addresses—all so you can scale like a legend. If you're ready to make moves, hit me up—I'll hook you up with a tiger team that's both ferocious and cost-effective.

Pro Tip: If you're going the Upwork route, nail down a killer SOP (Standard Operating Procedure). Spell precisely what you want in an "instructions" document, click-by-click, with screenshots and maybe a joke or two for good measure. Trust me, it'll save everyone much time and make scaling less of a headache.

Cohorts & Courses–Expand Without Cannibalizing

Always, always start high when selling services. If your VIP 1:1 package is a cool $18,000, lead with that offer—no hesitation. From there, you can work with a small group, a cohort, or maybe even a neighbor's cat. But remember, every new tier means more marketing, so only go "pyramid" if you love talking about your stuff.

Building courses isn't a walk in the park—it's like dating a stripper: exciting at first, but soon you're knee-deep in drama, late nights, and questionable decisions. And the people ready to pay $997 for a course? They're not the ones committing to high-ticket programs. Coaches waste months perfecting $1K courses, only to realize they could've landed a $12-25K client with way less effort and no glitter to clean up.

Here's the deal: courses and cohorts *can* be cash cows. Fast revenue, baby—I once pulled in $25K in a few days. The catch? Saturated markets and clients saying, "I've already learned everything in your course from your books," or worse, "I'm drowning in five other courses." Turns out, not everyone wants to binge-watch fifty canned videos like it's the latest season of *Project Runway*. Shocking, right? Attention spans are shorter than Trump's list of "great people, the best people" before he fires them.

That's where premium 1:1 options come in. Some coaches throw out black card offers, like $12-18K packages—and guess what? The ones who want it, *want it*. It bridges the gap beautifully, offering tailored 1:1 sessions at $250 to $2,000/hour. Clients get the VIP experience without wondering, "Wait, am I making a Tesla down payment?"

Fun fact: you can't lose a deal you never had. I've had clients start at $997 and later renew for $12,000—it happens more often than you think. And just a handful of $10K/month retainer clients? That's $30K a month or $360K a year. A few solid yeses, and you're laughing all the way to the bank.

That's the funny thing about this racket—it's like *The Hangover*. One yes, and you're partying in the penthouse with a tiger in the bathroom. One no, and you're waking up on the roof with no pants and a splitting headache.

On your way to $25K/month, think like Danny Ocean: smooth, sharp, and one step ahead. Anchor high, lock in premium 1:1 clients and snag a few team packages. Building the "perfect course" or running ads? That's betting it all on red and hoping Terry Benedict doesn't have cameras. Ads cost $150 per lead, and refunds? Yeah, right.

I once watched a startup burn $1MM on ads. The big score? One sad box of cupcakes from the agency. No cash, no jewels—just frosting and existential regret. Play it smart, keep it lean, and walk out like you cracked the Bellagio vault—because telling disappointed clients, "You shook Sinatra's hand," won't save the day.

CONCLUSION

Wisdom from Nightingale & Costanza

Whatever you've been told, whatever rule you've heard about "how to succeed"—flip it on its head. Earl Nightingale was right: if everyone's rushing one way, the real treasure is probably stashed in the opposite direction. You're here because you're ready to ditch the predictable, the same ol' sales scripts and "proven frameworks" and instead dive into the uncharted. After all, empires, fortunes, and dynasties weren't built by following the crowd. They were built by visionaries who took wild leaps and backed them up with guts.

Client acquisition, my friend, is older than pyramids. Fire-for-food old. Back then, if you had a fire, people listened. Fast forward to now, and we're flooded with all these so-called "growth hacks" and "guaranteed formulas." Well, I'm here to strip away the fluff, hand you a playbook, and remind you that creating clients is more straightforward than all the smoke and mirrors suggest. It's about listening, genuine curiosity, and, believe it or not, letting silence do the heavy lifting.

Listen, Jonny Staker, one of my clients, nailed it. After closing a $12K deal, another coach asked him, "What's your secret?"

And he replied, "I didn't talk." It wasn't the PowerPoint deck; it wasn't the razzle-dazzle. It was good old-fashioned listening. Silence? That's the undercover power play right there.

If you're here thinking, "But this space is too crowded!" let me tell you something: there's room for *you*. When I shifted my focus from profit to purpose, stopped performing, and started connecting, it was like the universe handed me a set of X-ray glasses. I could see what others missed. I want this Matrix vision for you. I want you to feel what it's like when clients choose you because, for once, they feel *seen*.

Five years ago, I was grinding, getting by, questioning everything. Today, I've built a globally recognized business, and I'm here telling you it's not just possible—it's inevitable if you want it badly enough. I want you to feel the thrill of hitting your first $25K month, buying that house, writing that book, and whatever wild dreams you've stashed away. This is about unleashing your full potential—the kind of big, bold moves that make you pause and say, "Wait... is this really my life?"

And let's be honest: statistically, I shouldn't be here. I should've been knocked off course long ago. But here I am, urging you to trust the words in these pages, the process, the systems, and—most importantly—yourself. When a client recently asked, "Does this stuff work?" I just said, "Trust me." And guess what? He closed his first $3K deal by breakfast the next day. That's the power of this.

The legends of my journey—my first VP of Sales, Jim Thoeni, Steve Hardison, "The Ultimate Coach"—all left me with these mantras I now pass on to you. Jim's was simple but potent: KTFB—Keep The Fire Burning. Let that fire guide you when the road is steep, rejection stings, and you're tempted to pack it in.

And as Steve Hardison always says at the end of everything: *Loving you.* So I say it to you now—thank you for letting me be part of this wild ride. Go out there and make magic, Mav.

Oh, and if you're ever in doubt? Take it from Jerry Seinfeld and George Costanza:

Jerry: If every instinct you have is wrong, then the opposite would have to be right.

George: Yes, I will do the opposite!

So, do the opposite. Do something. Do everything. And then get ready to watch your life explode into everything you ever wanted.

Vaya con dios!
— JM —

Acknowledgement

Thank yous:

Huge thanks to Charles Needham—RevOps wizard, rising star, and certified typo hitman—for saving this book from becoming a "flat" grammar crime scene. And to Mendy Zimmerman, sales polymath, and wisdom dealer, your edits on 3.0 and 4.0 were so sharp they should come with a warning label. Honestly, this book would've been a dumpster fire with a glossary without you two. Grateful doesn't even begin to cover it!

Aaron Barkman, Aaron Norris, Aaron Ross, Abhinav Gokllani, Abraham Orden, Aiko Aida, Alex Pehar, Andrew Richards, Ankush Jain, Anthony Iannarino, Art Sobczak, Austin Burson, Benjamin Dennehy, Benjamin Misner, Ben Sardella, Billy Sturgis, Bill Wacker, Bob Burg, Brandon Clauser, Brian Q. Davis, Brian Weber, Bruce Runions, Bryan Franklin, Cameron Rochette, Carlos Grimaldos, Carolyn Freyer-Jones, Charles H. Green, Charles Needham, Chris Caldwell, Chris Grosse, Chris Hopfer, Chris Rocas, Chris Russell, Chris Seidel, Christian Krause, Christian Retek, Cory Bray, Dale Dupree, Daniel Hebert, Daniel Mawad, Dario Junk, Darren Bullivant, David Bayer, David Creel, David Lichtenstein, Dennis Hettema, Dennis O'Hagan, Donal O'Riordan, Doug Rendler, Draper Donley, Edward van der Kleijn, Elijah Awoke, Elliott Hamrick, Eric Offner, Eric Steeves, Erich Neutze, Florian Decludt, Frank

Kohn, Fred Fox, Garrett C. MacDonald, Gavin Tice, Greg Larsen, Greg Meyer, Guido Klausbruckner, Gunnar Habitz, Haris Halkic, Ian Koniak, Jack Canfield, Jack Michel, Jakob Bysewski, James Khoury, James Ski, Jamal Reimer, Jamil Mahmood, Jason Erdes, Jason Sanders, Jeff Hassemer, Jeff Meyers, Jeff Thull, Jeremy Jones, Jim Holden, Jim Horning, Jim Mongillo, Jim Thoeni, Joey Gilkey, Joey Nanai, John Montgomery, John Patrick Morgan, John Welch, Jonny & Marlena Staker (thank you for the fighter plane design!), Joshua Pearson, Josh Bruer, Josh Norris, Josh Piepmeier, Judah Johns, Julia Nimchinski, Karen Davis, Karen Kelly, Karan Sharma, Kathleen Cameron, Kevin Casey, Kevin Dorsey, Kevin Hayler, Kieran Krohn, Luke Harris, Luke Shalom, Lylle Ryals, Mahan Khalsa, Malua Kamu, Marc Periou, Mario Krivokapic, Mark Raffan, Marylou Tyler, Matthew Mercer, Matthew Wayne Hoffman, Matt Evans, Matt Smyth, Matt Swain, Meadow Lacy, Melissa Ford, Mendy Zimmerman, Michael Koory, Michael Neill, Michael Versluis, Michal Bezak, Mike Bosworth, Mike Gallegos, Mike Milewski, Mike Weinberg, Moritz Aemisegger, Nate Stoltenow, Naveer Madni, Nejc Škoberne, Nick Zagar, Nikola Strah, Noel Coleman, Pascal Hippman, Patrick Thorp, Patrick Tinney, Paul M. Caffrey, Paul Vorsmann, Per Björnehammar, Peter Daneels, Peter McCammon, Peter Strauss, Phil Neil, Phil Smith (Illustration), Puneet Lamba, Quirein te Roller, Randy Stackaruk, Ranjan Kumar, Rhonda Byrne, Rich Evans, Rich Habets, Rich Litvin, Richard Asovia, Richard Lopez, Ronny Jensen, Sam Hull, Scott Leese, Scott Martinis, Sean Mulhern, Shane Palladino, Steve Bried, Steve Chandler, Steve Hardison, Steve Richard, Steve Shaw, Steven Brady, Stu Heinecke, TJ Allison, Tim Dodd, Todd Caponi, Tom Tobin, Tony J. Hughes, Townsend Wardlaw, Travis Brown, Travis Carter, Warren Lentz, Wes Schaeffer, Zach Scannapieco, Zach Selch.

About The Author

Justin Michael is a world-record-breaking, outbound sales maven who has arguably built the deepest client acquisition methodology of all time: the Justin Michael Method (*JMM*™). It's driven over 1B in pipeline for 200+ startups he's advised and over 25K reps, 1K of which he's personally coached. With 20+ years in sales, ex-Salesforce, and LinkedIn, Justin is the global authority on AI-based outbound prospecting alongside legends like Aaron Ross, Josh Braun, and Mark Roberge. His counterintuitive, mobile-responsive, neuroscience-backed visual prospecting methodology made him a million-dollar earner and helped countless startups scale past ten million dollars ARR. His clients frequently 2-5X their pipeline and income, consistently getting promoted within six months. Justin is the bestselling author of "Sales Superpowers" and "Tech-Powered Sales," which proved that over 75% of top funnel can be automated by raising your technology quotient (TQ). He lives in Los Angeles, California, advising top SaaS technology CROs and teams on bleeding-edge revenue models.

Learn more at SalesSuperpowers.com.

Made in the USA
Middletown, DE
23 February 2025